FAITH
FOR ALL
SEASONS

JEFF LUCAS

CWR

To Kay
Still the kindest person I've ever met

Contents

Introduction –
A man just like us

With a sudden 'plop', the envelope landed on the door mat.

It's a sound I welcome. These days, so-called 'snail mail' (that isn't junk) is rare.

Are you like me when it comes to letters? I love the delicious sound of mail being thrust through the letterbox. It's a sound guaranteed to motivate me to forsake the warmth of my bed and rush downstairs to gather up the daily prize. But as I picked up the envelope and examined it for some clue as to its contents (which is much more fun than just ripping the thing open, though slightly less logical), my heart sank.

Printed in lurid red letters were just two words.

No, they were not *Past Due*.

The words, '*Victory Report!*' screamed at me.

This was a familiar and unwelcome letter.

It arrived with monthly monotony – a newsletter from a nationally-known evangelist. The epistle had a threefold purpose. It provided points for prayer, showed photographs of the man himself (preaching, laughing, crying, walking his dog and smiling at his wife) and then it told me how to send money and exactly why I should send it, immediately, *right now!*

None of these things particularly troubled me: the man had integrity and a powerful ministry, and even the high-pressure sales technique didn't bother me too much.

What seriously jarred me was the fact that every report, month after month, was a *victory* report.

As I stood there, I thought how it would be more authentic (but less lucrative) to receive an envelope headed 'Defeat Report'. Not as exciting or sensational, but certainly a little more reflective of reality. How wonderful it would be to receive a defeat report, just once.

In the words of my friend Adrian Plass, some people are terminally addicted to being positive, and are probably bristling at my apparent negativity. But I'm not a defeatist. I'm uneasy in the company of those dour-faced negative Christians who vote against joy, noise, fun or, for that matter, victory, while maintaining a facial expression that communicates pure, sacred constipation.

But I do have a problem with the unreality of the monthly 'bliss bulletin', the notion that some Christians (particularly the famous types) breeze effortlessly through life in a constant state of blessed ecstasy, and that everything they touch, spiritually speaking, turns to gold or, in this case, victory.

The truth is that good Christians, even great Christians, experience times when life is painful, boring, or confusing.

General William Booth, founder of the Salvation Army, came to a place of total defeat more than once. His heavy itinerant ministry, with the accompanying loneliness that extensive travelling brings, caused him to write an epistle of lament to his wife Catherine:

> *I wonder whether I could not get something to do in London of some kind, some secretaryship or something respectable that would keep us going. I know how difficult*

*things are to obtain without friends or influence, as I
am fixed. But we must hope against hope, I suppose.*[1]

We should not be disappointed with the knowledge that even
history-makers like Booth struggled. Knowing that even the great
General went through these feelings is encouraging. Perhaps
that's why the Bible is so honest, providing us with stark portraits
of real, flesh-and-blood human beings who laughed and cried,
believed and doubted, walked in holiness and smeared their lives
with immorality. Scripture never presents us with a casebook of
grinning, larger-than-life heroes. Even the most prominent are
shown without theatrical makeup. Samson, anointed mighty
warrior, who overthrew hordes of Philistines, was conquered by
the lethal combination of a large ego and raging hormones. Peter,
key spokesman in the Early Church, whose shadow brought
instantaneous healing, was also the one who had walked
around with his mouth in fifth gear and his brain in neutral, until
finally the sound of the rooster crowing silenced his boasting.

The Bible never whitewashes failure – or defeat. Paul the apostle
was one of those stressed-out saints, and he did rather well as
a believer, to say the least. A third of the New Testament flowed
from his pen. Abundant miracles punctuated his life. He took day
trips to heaven, 'caught up in the Spirit' as he put it, but, because
he never lost touch with reality, he still knew how to draft a defeat
report. Writing to the contentious Corinthians, he bared his heart:

*We do not want you to be uninformed, brothers and
sisters, about the troubles we experienced in the province
of Asia. We were under great pressure, far beyond
our ability to endure, so that we despaired of life itself.
Indeed, we felt we had received the sentence of death.*
(2 Cor. 1:8–9, NIV)

That's straight talk. Imagine receiving a newsletter like that
today. 'Greetings, beloved prayer partners and financial

supporters. We want you to know the truth. We're fed up. Life has been a pain this month. We can't take much more of this. In fact, we're just a bit suicidal. Yours sincerely...

Jeremiah was another serious realist who often experienced wildly fluctuating emotions. Jeremiah 20:13 reveals a prophet on an emotional rollercoaster:

> *Sing to the LORD! Give praise to the LORD! He rescues the life of the needy from the hands of the wicked.*

That's positive enough. But now consider the very next verses:

> *Cursed be the day I was born! May the day my mother bore me not be blessed! Cursed be the man who brought my father the news, who made him very glad, saying, 'A child is born to you – a son!' May that man be like the towns the LORD overthrew without pity. May he hear wailing in the morning, a battle cry at noon. For he did not kill me in the womb, with my mother as my grave, her womb enlarged for ever. Why did I ever come out of the womb to see trouble and sorrow and to end my days in shame?*
>
> (Jer. 20:14-18, NIV)

This is the cry of a man of great faith and faithfulness – yet a man in turmoil, angry, disorientated, and in deep despair.

And so we come to Elijah.

What a mighty man he was.

His name means 'Yahweh – He is the real God.'

In merely introducing himself, Elijah made a powerful statement about the convictions that burned in his heart and were the foundations for his life. He was a seasoned veteran of faith, not an unstable novice. He experienced more of the raw power of God than most of us will ever see.

Elijah spoke to death, and death died, as he raised up a bitter widow's son.

He addressed the clouds and commanded them to hold back the rain – and they obeyed.

Fire leapt out of heaven at his word. One man against 450.

Elijah planted his feet, standing fearlessly before the highest authority in the land, the king and queen of Israel. He pointed a prophetic finger accusingly at the evil pair – 'You are the cause of all the trouble in Israel!' (1 Kings 18:17-18, my paraphrase).

But it was this same hero who, despite his calling and undeniable anointing from God, became so fearful and lonely that he prayed for death.

Elijah had a faith for all seasons. But faith is not a steady, consistent pulse. Faith fluctuates, grows, weakens, yet hopefully ends well. The journey of faith does not follow a straight line, always heading upward and onward. Faith usually hikes a zig-zagging, uncertain trail. Faith surges and fades. We will see that in Elijah's trek, in his glorious ministry which climaxed at Carmel, and in his time of defeat as he sat in a lonely cave pitted into the hillside of Mount Sinai.

As we trace his journey, I pray that we'll find the relief and liberation that this reality brings.

May I ask a kindness? Please don't skip over the biblical text and go right to the chapters. There is surely power in simply reading the story, allowing it to speak for itself, before considering any further comment about it.

Also, it's important to say that, while the core of this book is firmly based on what the biblical text says, there are times when I have allowed my imagination to flesh out the story a little. When I picture a petulant king Ahab stomping around his palace in a right royal strop, I am painting a picture that I think the Bible might imply rather than specifically describe. I hope that this creative approach to the narrative will help bring colour and clarity to the story.

I've delved into Elijah's story in three previously published books. I have now revised, updated and expanded on the exploration of his incredible story in this book – offering a fresh perspective on this timeless tale and what it can teach us.

If you come to this book while in a season of sadness or struggle, I pray that you'll be comforted by the knowledge that you're not alone.

I pray that you'll see afresh a God who doesn't always choose to answer all of our questions, but who is big enough to help us through the days of defeat. In his despair, Elijah wasn't sent packing by God. Rather, as we will see, he was gently recharged and recommissioned, and returned to blessing and usefulness. Scripture honours him greatly. More is written of him in the New Testament than of any other prophet, with the exception of Moses.

Only two human beings have not tasted death. Enoch was one of them, Elijah the other.

Who appeared on the Mount of transfiguration, conversing with Jesus before the harrowing hours of the cross?

Moses. And Elijah.

And it's worth noting that the Jewish people hold Elijah in incredibly high esteem:

> *At the observance of the Passover, orthodox Jews leave*
> *the door open so that Elijah may enter if he should*

suddenly come. Also orthodox Jews reserve a vacant
chair for Elijah at the circumcision of a child. And
some Jews honour Elijah in that when lost goods are
discovered and the owner cannot be found, they are
set aside until Elijah comes to identify the owner.[2]

It was David who testified that God 'restored his soul'.
The phrase is enlightening, because 'restore' is a shepherding
word, and David, because of his working background, used it
advisedly. Sometimes sheep go to sleep in hollows, and they
roll over on their backs, which renders them totally immobile
– and helpless. Unless the vigilant shepherd spots them in
their plight and comes to their aid, they will quickly drown
in their own lung fluids. Struggling and kicking, they wait for
help – or death. Hopefully, the shepherd will come and 'restore'
them – a gentle but firm nudge that will roll them back over.

Perhaps, like Elijah, life has dealt you some
unexpected blows lately, and you've had enough.
You're down and feel like you're almost out.

I pray that as we trace Elijah's steps for a while, you
will meet a God who can nudge us into light and life
again. May we discover that the God of Elijah is our God
too, and that we can be graced with a faith, not only
for the sunnier days, but for every season of life.

A faith for all seasons.

Jeff Lucas
Colorado 2016

[1] Harold Begbie, *The Life of William Booth* (London: MacMillan, 1926), p422

[2] J. G. Butler, *Elijah: The Prophet of Confrontation* Volume 3 (Clinton, IA: LBC Publications, 1994), p10

One:
BEGINNINGS

'Ahab son of Omri began to rule over Israel in the thirty-eighth year of King Asa's reign in Judah. He reigned in Samaria twenty-two years. But Ahab son of Omri did what was evil in the LORD's sight, even more than any of the kings before him. And as though it were not enough to follow the sinful example of Jeroboam, he married Jezebel, the daughter of King Ethbaal of the Sidonians, and he began to bow down in worship of Baal. First Ahab built a temple and an altar for Baal in Samaria. Then he set up an Asherah pole. He did more to provoke the anger of the LORD, the God of Israel, than any of the other kings of Israel before him.

It was during his reign that Hiel, a man from Bethel, rebuilt Jericho. When he laid its foundations, it cost him the life of his oldest son, Abiram. And when he completed it and set up its gates, it cost him the life of his youngest son, Segub. This all happened according to the message from the LORD concerning Jericho spoken by Joshua son of Nun.' – 1 Kings 16:29–34

Sweat glossed the woman's contorted face, a mask
of pain, her eyes sunken hollows in the candlelight,
a low moan now with each new contraction.

She was quite spent – not an ounce of energy
left – but the midwife who fussed around her bed
urged her on: just one last terrible push.

In the flickering shadows sat two other women, family
friends, muttering their commentaries, experts in their
own eyes at least. Minutes earlier the humble bedchamber
had reverberated with the woman's cries, her frantic
begging for it all to be over. But now she was too tired
even to cry out – she had to be delivered of this baby
now. Another few minutes and she would surely die.

Outside the house sat her husband; nervous, waiting.
He had steeled himself during the screaming, but now
the sudden quiet alarmed him more. He couldn't go
inside to check; it was unheard of, unthinkable.

So he waited alone.

How they wanted this baby now. When they had
first discovered the pregnancy, they had panicked.
There would be one more mouth to feed, and
times were hard for the likes of them.

Israel was experiencing something of a booming
economy – for the rich. The wealthy landowners
seemed possessed with a demonic greed, demanding
more and more rent from the tenant farmers until
there was just nothing left to fill empty bellies.

How would they manage?

But as the months had gone by and the child had enlarged in
the womb, so grew a strange sense of peace in their hearts.

They were both loyal followers of the true God. Not for them the dark foolishness of the Baals. Whatever the royal family was up to, whatever the rich folk worshipped, they would stay true to Yahweh. And as they prayed, so there came a sense that somehow, in a way they couldn't begin to explain, Yahweh Himself was involved in the birth of this child.

The thought was staggering.

It would appear to some as outrageous, pretentious for such ordinary folk to consider, but they had held it in their hearts; comfort for the future. As the man sat and pondered the silence that had fallen on the house, he prayed out loud: 'Lord of hosts! Give me a son.'

Suddenly the silence was shattered. Not this time by another scream, but by laughter and excited chatter. The child was here!

Without waiting to be asked, casting propriety to the wind, he rushed inside, and was immediately shocked to see the condition of his wife, her hair lank, her thighs bloodied; perhaps death was on her. And then she managed the faintest of smiles: it seemed that all was well.

The child was put to the breast, and immediately fresh energy seemed to surge into the woman. The midwife spoke: 'Give praise to your God... He's given you a son.'

The man smiled broadly, and ran his palm gently over his wife's fevered forehead, pushing back a hair that had strayed into the corner of her eye.

Now it was time to name this boy, this son of his. They had talked and laughed and prayed about it over and over these last few months, and they both knew the answer. If the Lord gave them a boy, then the lad would be known by a name that would publicly honour the true God. Such an act was dangerous. It was like thumbing a nose at the palace; an insulting slap in the face of the so-called gods. But the name had been chosen, and they would not go back on their decision.

They would go public with their allegiance to the Lord.

The name had a meaning: 'The Lord – He is the real God.'

Eli-yah.

Elijah.

–   –   –   –   –

Gilead was a place of striking, rugged scenery; beautiful to share, terrifyingly quiet for the lonely traveller.

The Jordan River separated Gilead from the rest of Israel, both geographically and culturally. Thick, shaggy forests covered the hillsides – lush land where large herds of sheep grazed, and mountain streams skipped and trickled down.

Towering cliffs began in limestone and were peaked in black volcanic rock.

The prophets sang about its picturesque views; the sick clamoured for its famous spice, the balm of Gilead, which was reputed to ease pain.

The locals, like their land, were separate and proud. They looked with disdain at those who farmed beyond the Jordan, sneered at them as compromisers, lovers of the Baals. Many of them lived and worked in the open air – tough, serious shepherds.

They lived in black Bedouin goat-hair tents, clumped together in makeshift villages, enabling them to live in the heights during summer and move to the valleys in wintertime. Dressed in camel-hair cloaks held together by thick, crude leather belts, they made a stark contrast to the sophistication of the city-dwellers, and the affluent finery of those privileged enough to be part of the Royal Samaritan Court.

Even their speech set them apart, talking with such a strong accent that in times of war they distinguished friend from foe simply by asking them to say one word: 'Shibboleth' (Judg. 12:5–6). The uninitiated enemy, unable to imitate the dialect, was discovered within seconds.

Elijah was born approximately 2,900 years ago in Gilead, in the little town of Tishbe. It was not an auspicious place for a great man to begin his life. Tishbe was so obscure that archaeologists can't even tell us its exact location.

–　　　–　　　–　　　–　　　–

All was far from well in the nation.

For many years Israel had been rotting in serious moral and spiritual decay, and by the time Elijah had reached adulthood, they had come to an all-time low – the bottom of the pit.

The golden age of David and Solomon was over. Six kings had come and gone in just 58 years – a royal rogues' gallery.

The first two of were idolaters.

The third was a murderer. After that came a ruler who was an alcoholic *and* a murderer.

Number five was accused of 'spiritual treason', and the sixth, incredibly, was described as worse than the previous five.

Now the seventh king was on the throne, and he beat even number six in being an expert in evil.

He was Ahab; his wife was the infamous Jezebel.

It is unlikely that their marriage was truly happy, because it was the fruit of shrewd politics rather than real love.

Ahab and Jezebel came together as a result of a peace treaty struck by Ahab's father, Omri, with the Phoenicians in the north. Omri was a brilliant tactician. He came to power after four years of raging civil war in Israel, when the army and the ruling classes had been at loggerheads. Omri had held the loyalty of the military. Tibni, son of Ginath, was the darling and hero of the ruling classes, but Omri had prevailed and become King.

Now it was time for strength and consolidation, and an alliance with the powerful Phoenicians seemed good for everyone. Both Israel and Phoenicia were under threat from the Syrians, so a co-operative treaty appeared to make a great deal of sense.

Terrible choices often appear to be perfectly logical.

To seal the deal, young Prince Ahab was given in marriage to Princess Jezebel, daughter of Eshbaal, the priest-king of Tyre, a massively powerful nation which even had colonies in faraway Europe.

The marriage was totally forbidden by the law of God, but who was worried?

Integrity was sacrificed daily on altars of convenience: the union of Ahab and Jezebel was good for both countries – or so it seemed.

It is uncertain whether Jezebel wed Ahab as the already reigning king or when he was still crown prince. All we know for sure is that the marriage took place between 878 and 872 BC; Ahab ruled as king during 874–853 BC. And what is certain is that the rule of Ahab and Jezebel cast a deep, dark shadow over Israel – a 21 year season of death.

When Jezebel moved house and home to Samaria to begin a new life, she brought her fascination with the occult with her. Jezebel was a devoted, perhaps fanatical worshipper of Baal Melqart, the chief god of Tyre (the name Melqart means 'king of the city', a territorial principality). Baal worship was nothing new to Israel – they had long been worshipping Baals – but the arrival of the Princess Jezebel of Tyre marked the beginning of a new era of idolatry.

Foreign queens were commonly allowed to practice their own religion. Solomon's wives had littered the western slopes of the Mount of Olives with their occultic shrines, but this had no real effect on the general population – theirs was a private indulgence.

But Jezebel was different. Evangelical in her occultic zeal, she had a huge temple erected in honour of Melqart, and then began to turn on those who insisted that Yahweh alone was God. She was a mass-murderess who nursed a pathological hatred for anything to do with Yahweh, establishing a programme of wholesale execution for God's prophets. By the time Ahab became king, Jezebel had built up a full-time staff of 450 Baal prophets, plus an extra team of four hundred prophets of the goddess Asherah. She was a clever opportunist, the real source of power in the land.

Baal worship was far more than an alternative theory, an occult philosophy. It was an active, energetic pulse of evil that became hugely popular with the masses.

It's not hard to see why Baalism was enjoying a revival, quite apart from the credibility that came with royal patronage.

Baal worship played on the depraved human hunger for occult power and perverse sex.

The idea that God – or the gods – can be bought or bribed has always been attractive to arrogant humanity. That is why some people would far rather whip themselves, put needles into their bodies or drag themselves up a shrine hill on their knees, than accept God's scandalous offer of free forgiveness. Human pride loves to pay – it feeds our sense of self-sufficiency. Baal, therefore, was a hired hand-god: give the right offering, friend, and all will be well with you and yours. Your cosmic insurance premium will be paid up, and disaster won't come near you. Even if you have to cut yourself with knives in the process (as Baal prophets often did), it will be worth it all in the end, because you'll get your heart's desire.

Worshippers of Baal also believed that the gods (who were obviously slow on the uptake) needed humans to act out their prayerful instructions in order to get the message through. This was a society that heavily relied on agriculture, so a bumper harvest was a priority. Baal was supposed to have power over drought and sterility, so the dramatic prayer followed logically: 'Listen, Baal, we need you to help our seeds to be fertilised, and in case you're not sure what it is we're asking for, here are a few dozen shrine prostitutes, male and female, acting out a fertility ritual just to make it absolutely clear.'

The third and most hideous facet of the Baal cult was child sacrifice. It beggars belief that any mother would allow her newborn child to be taken, warm from the breast, and then watch it be thrown into a blazing furnace.

Misguided religion is a terrible curse.

Queen Jezebel was no stranger to death: her own father had acquired power in Tyre because he had taken on the role of political assassin. According to the historian Josephus, Jezebel's father had been a long-time priest of Astarte who had murdered his brother, King Phelles, ascending to the throne at the age of 36. Her father's name gives an interesting insight to the wholehearted commitment of this evil family to the occult: it simply means 'with Baal'. The atmosphere of her childhood was an ideal environment to foster a psychopathic temperament. For as long as she could remember, human life had been cheap. This then was the religion of Jezebel: arrogant, pornographic and running with the blood of the innocents.

Ahab, however, was a completely different character from his wife.

A moral weakling, he was a man who lacked conviction and decisiveness. He didn't even share his bride's single-minded commitment to the Baals. In fact, it would seem that Ahab was incapable of being single minded about anything. He was just willing to worship whomever and whatever, as long as it kept everybody happy. Ever the man to please, Ahab had himself set up a special sacred stone monument to the Baals near to the altar of the occultic temple and, just to be on the safe side, he threw in a pole in honour of goddess Asherah for good measure.

He even named three of his children in honour of Yahweh – Jehoram ('Yahweh is high'), Ahaziah ('Yahweh has taken hold') and Athaliah ('Yahweh is exalted'). Ahab was a man of religious tokenism, willing to treat the God of heaven and the devil of hell like good luck charms, to use and discard at will. Sometimes his carelessness backfired. Years earlier, Joshua had put a curse on the city of Jericho, and had decreed that anyone who tried to rebuild it would be hit by the loss of their children. Scripture records that a man named Hiel attempted to flout the warning and go ahead with a construction programme anyway, which he did 'in the time of Ahab'. That little phrase means that it was done with Ahab's knowledge, even perhaps decreed by Ahab, as Jericho was right on a major trade route. Never mind what the man of God had said in the past. Ahab didn't have to risk anything personally anyway. It was Hiel's head – and the heads of his children – that were on the block, and it was he who ultimately suffered judgment.

In the Walt Disney cartoon film *Robin Hood*, the evil Prince John is portrayed as a skinny lion who shouts and screams and wields absolute power, but sticks his thumb in his mouth and goes into a tantrum whenever life gets difficult. Ahab was such a character – one of those moody types who would sulk like a child when he didn't get his own way. On one occasion he was desperate to gain control of a vineyard in Jezreel, but the owner, Naboth, wouldn't strike a deal.

The great king's response?

> *So Ahab went home, sullen and angry because Naboth the Jezreelite had said, 'I will not give you the inheritance of my ancestors.' He lay on his bed sulking and refused to eat.*
> (1 Kings 21:4, NIV)

His immaturity and lack of moral backbone are further illustrated by the way he allowed himself to be shamelessly manipulated by his wife. Scripture provides a most pathetic epitaph:

> *There was never anyone like Ahab, who sold himself to do evil in the eyes of the LORD, urged on by Jezebel his wife.*
> (1 Kings 21:25, NIV)

When Naboth wouldn't co-operate, a simple 'frame-up' job was set in motion at the suggestion of conniving Jezebel, and this resulted in the execution of the unfortunate businessman.

Ahab, like a rich, spoilt brat who can only lust after other children's toys, was free to take possession of the vineyard.

So we have King Ahab and Queen Jezebel – enemies of God and His people – a manic pair, driven, unpredictable and ruthless, in tandem for Satan. As one writer puts it:

> *By himself Ahab would have been a menace… plainly an opportunist, he seemed to have few convictions or scruples. But he was not by himself. Jezebel was by his side, using her prestige and influence as insidiously and maliciously as possible. The corruption of Canaanite religion had long been seeping in from the Israelites' Canaanite neighbours, but under Jezebel it was pumped from the palace with extraordinary pressure.*[1]

Ahab ruled the land, but he was ruled by Jezebel, who in turn was ruled by the gods of blood and uncleanliness, Baal and Asherah.

But God had not abandoned the nation.

The Lord had His mole in the palace.

He was Obadiah, a high-ranking minister of state, who was in charge of the royal household.

Obadiah was the original double agent. Risking certain death if discovered, he set up a rescue programme, hiding a hundred of God's prophets away in caves, and keeping them supplied with food and water.

And God had a plan, the raising up of one very loud prophetic voice. Elijah.

-    -   -   -   -

It had been one of those long, balmy days that
often shape vivid childhood memories.

The two teenage lads, more men than boys now really,
had chased their way around a thousand rocks, dangled
their feet luxuriously in the cool mountain streams,
and now it was time to head for home: a good day.

The sun was slipping quickly behind distant Carmel.
Their bodies ached the pleasant ache of energy
spent, fun enjoyed. Their stomachs were hungry
for food, their limbs ready to melt into sleep.

Then, with just a mile to go, they heard the drums.

Immediately they knew. This was what father had warned
them about repeatedly. He had commanded them in no
uncertain terms to stay away from the evening feasts.
But curiosity drew them like a magnet, away from
father's wise words. Their minds made up, they began
to run towards the sound of the dull thudding.

They were perfectly safe in the lengthening
shadows of the rocks, yet later they both admitted
to being frozen to the spot with terror. A fierce,
angry fire tore with rage at the gathering dusk.

The figures of the Baal priests circled around it seemed
contorted – caught more in spasm than in dance, as they
stamped and screamed, round and round. Wide eyed,
the boys watched as the dancers, apparently mesmerised
by their magic and music, waved their arms high.

And then the boys found themselves blushing to
the very roots of their hair as members of the crowd
began to peel off their clothing and join in with the
writhing ritual. Men ran their hands greedily over
the bodies of women they had never met.

The shadows held no attraction; discretion was irrelevant. In the harsh glare of the fire, many were already locked in a loveless celebration of lust...

It went on for a long time.

The boys just knelt there, unable to speak, and occasionally they pushed their faces hard onto the rock to block out the gross images that stained the night. And then, just when they thought it was all over, and that all the evil was spent, they saw the woman, just a young girl really, standing with a bundle of cloth in her arms. She was nervous, shifting her weight from one foot to the other, waiting. Conflicting shadows of emotion raced across her face: one moment an expression of spiritual intensity, as she tried to enter into the worship – and then, the passion would suddenly fade, wiped off and replaced by a look of bewilderment, a little lost child face. At last, as if to settle the matter, her moment came. The gyrating priests broke their tortured circle and allowed her to step in. The drums grew louder, and then suddenly, with one violent beat, everything stopped dead. The dancers seemed frozen to the spot; every one of them now gazing intently at the girl. And suddenly her eyes seemed like empty sockets. Tears stained her cheeks as very slowly she began to open the bundle of cloths.

Watching from the shadows, Elijah felt like his heart was going to stop beating. As the grubby cloths were unwrapped, he saw the pure skin of a baby, no more than a month old.

As if to urge the woman on, the music began again, louder, manic now. From deep within the woman came a long moan, the sound of a soul in torture, as she flung her child into the roaring flames. Mercifully, the music muffled the child's final screams, and the woman crumpled to the ground.

Elijah pounded the rock that sheltered him; tears mingled with anger and frustration.

And for him, innocence died with the child.

- - - - -

Perhaps it's the temptation of every generation.

We quickly buy the notion that things are going from bad to worse, that evil is increasing at such an unbearable rate, that there's little hope, nothing to be done, and that even faith cannot really fix the current maladies and tragedies that unfold all around us.

Certainly recent months have ushered in unprecedented uncertainties.

Brexit, and the political tsunami that followed it, with warnings of dire economic aftershocks to come. Hasty leadership reshuffles, and totally unexpected appointments.

The trauma of a man using a lorry to mow down helpless Bastille Day revellers, some of them tiny children – their now empty strollers a stark reminder of the heartless brutality of his zig-zagging death mission.

An attempted coup in Turkey, quickly stifled, but leaving an aftertaste of uncertainty in its wake. Slaughter in Afghanistan, Iraq, Florida.

Black lives not mattering too much in America, and the lives of innocent law enforcement officers killed in retaliation seeming to not matter much either.

Two candidates for the White House, leaving many feeling that they don't have confidence to really choose either one.

Things are going downhill fast.

It's a phrase I often hear from Christians. As we look around our terror-stricken world, where technology fuels our fear with HD-quality footage of brutal torture and executions, we assume that everything is getting worse.

Economic uncertainty, European turbulence, mistrust in politicians, an international refugee crisis – all of this stokes up the notion that the world must surely be coming to an end. Some even speculate that these events are not just signs of the times, but signs of the end times.

We can be tempted by the idea that faith is more difficult, maybe even well-nigh impossible, living in the days that we do.

But we're wrong. The world has been dimmed since Eden, and the first murder that followed shortly thereafter. Elijah lived out his faith in a culture where child sacrifice was the norm, where those who held the reins of power were unutterably evil, and where he stood as one of the persecuted few rather than the favoured majority.

Faith in his day was an uphill climb, a costly choice.

It was then. It is now.

But God was. And He still is.

Elijah lived out his story of faith during one of the darkest nights of Israel's history.

The ministry of Jesus mushroomed during a time when the land was occupied by Roman oppressors who levied crippling taxes, crucified any vocal opponents, placed a puppet king in place, and ruled with an iron fist.

Yet during those twilight years, the kingdom of God broke out in mighty power.

And it still can, because Caesar is not Lord, and neither is Mrs May, Donald Trump, Hillary Clinton. Vladimir Putin, or even that rather strange chap who dominates North Korea, Kim Jong-un.

Remember the name of that prophet again.

Eli-yah.

The Lord – He is the real God.

Jesus is *still* Lord.

[1] William Sanford LaSor, David Allen Hubbard, Frederic William Bush, *Old Testament Survey* (Grand Rapids, MI: William B. Eerdmans Publishing Co, 1982), p266

[2] J.G. Butler, *Elijah: The Prophet of Confrontation Volume 3* (Clinton, IA: LBC Publications, 1994), p24

Two:
FOUNDATIONS

'Now Elijah, who was from Tishbe in Gilead, told King Ahab, "As surely as the LORD, the God of Israel, lives—the God I serve—there will be no dew or rain during the next few years until I give the word!"' – 1 Kings 17:1

Encounter with God.

It's what all believers crave.

Authentic encounters make the theory of faith more solid, concrete even, because God Himself has interacted with us.

Perhaps it was out in the Gilead highlands that the young Elijah first became personally aware of the living God.

The campfire stories at the end of the day had played their part in influencing his thinking, but out there alone, with only the trickling of the mountain streams breaking the hot, still silence, he would walk and think and consider his life.

What young lad, alone out in the hills, has not called out his own name and clapped his hands just to hear the echo reply? But perhaps there was another name now that Elijah would call out, enjoying the sound of it bouncing around hillsides: 'Yahweh!'

And one day he sensed a reply that came, not echoing and booming around the hillsides, but from somewhere deep within himself. A voice seemed to be calling *his* name.

Rumours about the dark goings on at the palace had been hurriedly whispered behind cupped hands in the marketplace. But, as time went on, the picture became sickeningly clear – the disease had spread like an epidemic.

By now Israel was infested with Baal worship. Some had spoken out about the disgrace that was blighting the land. Perhaps the more earthy among them cracked unkind jokes about the beautiful Jezebel. She loved to paint her eyes with kohl, a primitive mascara mixture of burnt frankincense and almond shells. She was famous for her arched eyebrows and the jet-black lines that edged her eyelids.

But her name would have triggered a thousand private jokes.

In her own language, 'Jezebel' means 'Where is Baal?'
In Hebrew, 'Zebel' means 'refuse' or 'dung', the irony
of which would surely not have been lost on the
poor. 'She's powerful, she's pretty, but she's...'

Eventually, however, even the whispers of dissent would
have faded, hushed by the news that the Yahweh prophets
were being arrested and executed. At a religious level,
many of the people seemed blissfully unconcerned. After
all, wasn't Yahweh just another one of the Baals anyway?

But Elijah, by now a grown man, couldn't surrender
his heart and mind to that spiritual pragmatism.

What had began within him as a flickering, tiny flame
of anger and disgust at the apostasy of the people had
been steadily fanned into a raging furnace of fury. The
Spirit of God served as divine bellows, coaxing the
flames, urging them to rise and roar. But with the fresh
passion and indignation came a sense of helplessness.

What could he, just another country boy, do about the situation?

The answer was obvious, for it was the only answer – he could pray.

Probably the passion had begun with
prayer – most great things do.

And how he prayed. The book of James tells us that he prayed
'earnestly' – the exact translation is, 'He prayed in prayer'. This
was no hurried notelet to God, scrawled in between more
pressing and important engagements. This was a prayer
symphony of angry tears, whispers and shouts, strident walking
up and down, up and down, and a body pressed hard into
the earth, shoulders shaking, a fist hammering the ground; a
repetitive, dull thud as he pounded out his demands to God.

'Praying in prayer' is dangerous. Only those who mean business should try it, because it inevitably leads to radical action. Intercession is a bridge between interest and involvement. Prayer is a springboard, a trigger that really should carry a health warning. Prayer is risky, and may seriously affect our capacity for ease, comfort and general mediocrity.

'Praying with prayer' is focused, strategic praying too. Elijah knew the Law of God; he had read and reread those old words, and he knew that they were still true:

> *If you carefully obey the commands I am giving you today, and if you love the LORD your God and serve him with all your heart and soul, then he will send the rains in their proper seasons – the early and late rains – so you can bring in your harvests of grain, new wine, and olive oil. He will give you lush pastureland for your livestock, and you yourselves will have all you want to eat. But be careful. Don't let your heart be deceived so that you turn away from the LORD and serve and worship other gods. If you do, the LORD's anger will burn against you.* He will shut up the sky and *hold* back the rain, *and the ground will fail to produce its harvests.*
>
> (Deut. 11:13-17, my emphasis)

One phrase gripped his heart and wouldn't let go. 'He will... hold back the rain... he will hold back the rain... he will hold back...'

So, nervously at first, for it seemed such a terrible prayer, he began to ask for a divine drought. The more he prayed, the more logical the prayer seemed, for a drought would certainly be an attention-grabber. The common belief of the new, evil religion was that Baal was the god of rain (*Rkb 'rpt,* 'the Rider in the Clouds'), and that Baal lived in a house in the sky that had a 'rain window' in it. An ancient inscription has been found that celebrates this Ugaritic myth:

Let a window be opened in the house. An aperture in the midst of the palace. And let a cleft be opened in the cloud.

Another declared: 'Baal... makes his voice heard in the clouds, he shoots forth lightning, and sends the beneficent rain'.

Since Baal was now supposed to be the one who provided rain, the absence of it in a drought was believed to be the sign of the death of Baal, overcome by the god Mot, the god of death.

In every way, drought would be a loud and clear message from Yahweh. And so the asking turned into pleading, and then perhaps the pleading stopped and he found himself almost commanding God to do just what He had promised to do in the book of the Law. But even if and when drought came, would Ahab and Jezebel recognise the judgment of Yahweh, or would they just redouble their efforts and increase their Baal bribes, perhaps even switching allegiance to Mot? There was only one solution: someone would have to go into the palace and tell them.

–   –   –   –   –

Prayer.

Frankly, I simply don't understand how it works.

I know that God calls us to a relationship by faith, and that prayer is a part of experiencing that daily. It's not easy, talking to someone who is invisible, and who, most of the time, doesn't talk back. I hear those Christians – usually leaders – who describe their daily chats with the Creator of the universe, during which He apparently converses freely with them about all kinds of what mostly seem like trivial issues, and I am not sure whether to envy or question the authenticity of their spirituality.

But I get it that God wants us to talk with Him, and have moments when He might whisper to us.

The part that I don't understand is where we try to get as many people as possible to pray about a particular need or issue.

I saw it on Facebook just today. Someone's daughter is undergoing a major surgery. He is asking all who know him to join in prayer for her, and asking that the Facebook post be shared, to recruit more people who will pray.

I don't question that calling of the troops to pray. I've done it, and I'll do it again.

I just don't really understand the mechanics of the idea.

Imagine it. God is greeted by a junior angel, who advises Him that, through the wonders of social networking, 11,423 people have 'liked' a Facebook post, 8,420 have promised to pray for the need, and 6,325 have *actually* prayed (we often promise to pray, but don't deliver on the promise).

But 6,325 is just not enough, says the Lord. If Twitter can also be employed, and the number of people actually praying exceeds 10,000, then God will consider meeting that need and answering that prayer as requested. A meter installed in heaven will automatically update the angelic community with the numbers of intercessors as they come in, in real time.

I really don't think it works like that.

I believe that God has called His people to partner with Him in His unfolding actions on the earth. The call to prayer is a dignified call to take authority, to participate in the works of the kingdom of God on earth.

But beyond that, I don't understand it. But I'll still do it.

And then there's another challenge, a
question created by blessing.

We often think that it is *unanswered* prayer that
nudges us into difficulty and questioning.

But *answered* prayer creates its own questions. Put simply, when
God does something spectacular, perhaps unexpected, then
the question arises, if He did *this*, why did He not do *that*?

This dilemma arose in my own life just this last week.

I learned that a man had been wonderfully
healed during a service I was leading.

Now just to be clear, I don't have a healing ministry. On the
contrary, when I pray for people, they usually get worse.
Not only can I not claim any credit as the preacher who
was teaching on healing when this miracle happened,
but I'd suggest that God probably healed someone despite
me, and certainly not in any way because of me.

Billy came forward for prayer at the end of a service I
conducted four years ago. Battling prostate cancer, he had
decided to present himself to God and ask for help.

There had been no stirring testimonies shared, no certainty
of healing offered, no soaring chords from the worship
band to create the 'right' atmosphere. I just suggested to the
congregation that we simply ask God, and then leave it to Him.

Billy was prayed for by one member of the ministry team, and
then another. And then he just stood there while the worship
group quietly played. It was then that he heard a voice.

'What do you need?'

He responded as he had before, saying that he had a variety of health issues. The person who asked the question told him that he had but one health issue, and ministered to him.

Later, doctors declared that there was no cancer, no chemotherapy needed, no hormone therapy. Four years on, his healing remains.

Sharing his story to encourage others, the congregation clapped and cheered. Later a lady suffering from multiple sclerosis told me that she had lost all symptoms following prayer.

I don't doubt these wonderful instances of answered prayer, although I am utterly committed to ensuring that the medical profession confirm that healing has actually happened before any claims are made. God is not glorified by hopeful speculation or even innocent exaggeration. And I'm wary of those healing services where sufferers are prayed for and then a microphone is thrust at them, and they're asked if they're feeling better. With a thousand or more people hoping that you are better, almost willing you to be better, it's difficult to say that you're not. Prayer for healing demands good practice.

But even when healing is authenticated, or any other answer to prayer is shared, we come back to that other niggling question that will never go away this side of eternity.

God did this. Why didn't He do *that*?

Questions remain.

But even though we might feel hemmed in by question marks at times, the call to all of us is simple.

Let's pray.

Let's call others to join us.

Let's trust when the answer doesn't come.

And let's trust when it does come.

–   –   –   –   –

Perhaps it started as an idle daydream. We all
take those familiar and fantastic mental journeys
– ideas that we flirt with once in a while, and then
send packing with an embarrassed smile.

This daydream, however, wouldn't go away. And it was
always the same: he saw himself marching straight into
the inner chambers of the royal palace. He'd square
up, look the king straight in the eye and proclaim
the word of God in a calm, clear voice. It was a wild
notion that refused to be vaporised by reality.

And slowly the truth dawned. God was broadcasting
daydreams on Elijah's personal wavelength, quietly calling
him to be the answer to his own prayers. The God of all
Israel was looking for a divine messenger, with the palace
of Samaria as the first delivery point. Elijah took a deep
breath and prepared himself for the toughest challenge
of his life – his mission, if he chose to accept it.

Take time out for a moment, and imagine
what it could have been like.

You're going to stare down the highest power in the
land and give him a message that he will hate. One that
will make his murderous wife absolutely furious.

Think of the raw, stomach-clenching fear that would stiffen
every muscle in your body as you realised that you were in
a place where you were totally, utterly alone, and that every
living soul was an enemy. That's probably how Elijah felt as
he marched towards Samaria, the ominous outline of the
hilltop palace seeming both to summon and threaten him.

A slow, agonising death in the bowels of Ahab's palace was a very real possibility. He had heard the stories of how Ahab and Jezebel had treated Yahweh's few remaining prophets. They had been run through with the sword. What would it feel like, sharp metal ploughing through flesh, with the jeers of mocking guards the last sound in your ears as life drained from you? Or perhaps death would be a saviour, mercifully snatching him from the hands of grinning torturers; blackness ending his screams.

Hurriedly, Elijah shook off the clammy grip of fear and the horrifying images that crouched in a corner of his mind. He continued his walk, the royal city ever closer.

–   –   –   –   –

What kind of a person can look death in the face and still stay faithful to the mission? Elijah was no Jonah – a pensive, reluctant prophet dragged by the Spirit kicking and screaming, finally speaking up for God.

Elijah would have known the dangers but he still made the trip.

We reveal volumes about ourselves when we open our mouths. Out of the abundance of the heart the mouth speaks. A lot of Elijah's personality and character is revealed by the few sentences that he speaks to the king. I imagine that he had agonised over his message, every word scrutinised in prayer until it became, as one commentator puts it, 'a spiritual stun grenade'.

'As surely as the LORD, the God of Israel, lives – the God I serve – there will be no dew or rain during the next few years until I give the word!'

–   –   –   –   –

Elijah was blunt.

He had no false commitment to bland
niceness that some mistake for love.

He was bold – and brief. Prophets can say a great
deal with just a few hand-picked words.

Nathan yelled just one sentence: 'You are the
man!' and King David came tumbling down from
his royal high horse, his scheming and adultery
instantly exposed by the prophetic spotlight.

Elijah made no attempt at introduction or explanation
– this wasn't an occasion for subtlety or tact – so his
words stung. They were a shocking slap in the royal
face: 'In the name of Yahweh, the living God of Israel.'

Because of the spreading Baal epidemic, Yahwehism had
become something of an outdated tradition. At best it was a
doctrine from the past – only around seven thousand people
in the whole nation were still faithful to Yahweh – so the
consensus was that Yahweh was dead, and the Baals lived.

We've already seen that a succession of Israel's kings had
mocked Yahweh by their lifestyles, words and flirtations with
occultism. Yahweh had failed to respond with strategically
directed lightning bolts, or indeed any other act of retribution,
which fuelled the notion that He no longer existed. 'Not so!' says
Elijah. 'Yahweh is alive.' And the inference is obvious: 'The Baals
are the lifeless ones around here. They are images that can't
see or hear – wooden godlings compared to the living God.'

In many ways, modern society mirrors the 'Where
has God gone?' attitude of the ancients. I remember a
well-known international evangelist was interviewed
live on BBC breakfast television about a major
mission which was to take place in London.

The evangelist in question is a controversial figure, but I was intrigued to note the look of total disbelief and wide-eyed astonishment on the interviewer's face - and all because the Christian leader made the comment, without fanfare or fuss, 'God spoke to me'.

'Excuse me,' interrupted the man from the BBC. 'Did you say... God speaks to you?'

'Certainly,' was the reply.

'You mean... God speaks to you?'

'Absolutely.'

The camera zoomed onto the face of the interviewer to capture his expression. It was a look of pity. Many believe that talking to God - prayer - is a good idea. But the belief that He might talk back is often greeted with incredulity.

It seems God is allowed to exist as long as He doesn't speak, act, heal, or do anything else to interfere. 'If God isn't dead, then let Him remain distant,' is the prevailing attitude.

I think we can safely assume that Elijah would have treated the contemporary 'truth is whatever you want it to be' philosophy that plagues our culture with an equal amount of tactless scorn and derision. In a world where uncertainty is fashionable, we could use a few more prophets who are sure of their message and their God.

I'm not calling for crass arrogance here, or disrespect for those of other faiths.

But in a world where we can often feel completely paralysed by what seems to be an unhealthy obsession with political correctness, gracious confidence in the gospel is still vital.

Thirty years ago, the Church in the UK was struggling to come to terms with the fact that we are now a post-modern culture – there is no core story, no meta-narrative at the heart of things. The absence of a meaningful story to live by inevitably leads to an erosion of values – if there is no meaning, then there are no standards, except some inherent core values that linger.

Three decades later, we are wrestling with a liberal fundamentalism that is intolerant about any attitude that it perceives as intolerant! You can believe anything you like, as long as your beliefs don't conflict with the liberal consensus. We won't tolerate that, and if you step out of line, we'll brand you as intolerant! In a world awash with meaninglessness, we need to be prepared to quietly make our stand for this truth: in Christ alone, hope is found.

Of course, lest some take this act of bluntness as a licence to be rude and arrogant in Jesus' name, we'd do well to remember that Elijah stood unswervingly on the word that God had placed in his heart, and not on his own opinions and prejudices.

Having nailed his colours to the mast, Elijah drives his point deeper, for not only is Yahweh the God who lives, but He is the real God of Israel. No wonder Jezebel threw a fit.

In the midst of a nationwide occultic revival, Elijah plants a claim flag for God, who is not only the Lord of hosts, but the God of Israel too. He is the one who entered into covenant with Abraham and Moses, the real owner of the land.

The message was plain.

God, the real God, the only God – He lives.

Surely that should be the heart of the good news that *we* share.

Christianity is not just a vague belief system, or a series of ethical guidelines or commands that are helpful and healthy for everyday living, a moral code for decent people to follow.

Christianity is not just an insurance policy guaranteeing a destination in paradise in the afterlife.

The Christian faith centres around a cross, and a tomb that has been vacated, because Jesus is alive, the only One who has beaten the power of death, and therefore has authority over all matters to do with life.

Our greatest enemy, the grave, is defeated. Everything is different.

The Lord has risen!

-        -   -   -   -

'As surely as the LORD, the God of Israel, lives – the God I serve – there will be no dew or rain during the next few years until I give the word!'

Elijah knew who God was – and he knew who he was *in God* too.

Humanly speaking, he was an obscure nobody from the hills of Gilead, a country bumpkin without the benefit of social pedigree or standing.

Scruffy in his peasant's garb, prophesying to a man dripping gold and bedecked in the finest clothes, he could have so easily shrivelled with intimidation – a little man hopelessly out of his league.

And let's be clear – Elijah was just a man. Some Jewish tradition suggests that Elijah was an angel, for only an extra-terrestrial could have done the exploits he did. Such a suggestion is theft, for this is a story of God being glorified through human weakness, water turned to wine, the ordinary becoming sacred. 'Elijah was a human as we are,' insists James (James 5:17).

But he was a man with a sense of God-given identity, which had nothing to do with social climbing or designer clothing. He was the servant of the Lord, who, as one translator puts it, 'stood before God'.

The term speaks of serving, of being ready, and also of standing in an intimate friendship: all three are vital components of a healthy relationship with God.

So Elijah stood before two kings: one a powerful but pathetic imitation of manhood; the other the King of kings and Lord of lords, a powerful friend to have when you're dancing with death.

Only a human secure in their own identity could deliver the message that Elijah brought, which would have infuriated Ahab at every level. The weather forecast itself was bad – very bad. For three-and-a-half years the 'sky was shut up', as Jesus Himself later described it, and as James confirmed in his epistle.

That was a massive blow for prosperous, thriving Israel. Even Ahab's political marriage to Jezebel from powerful Tyre couldn't save the nation from the famine that was to follow.

There were other implications too. Many regarded Baal as the god of the sun. Yet Baal worshippers believed that Baal controlled the rain as well and was responsible for abundant crops – so the message was doubly damning.

And then his final phrase was almost certainly guaranteed to send Ahab into apoplexy, as Elijah announced: 'The sky is shut – until I open it.'

If we are going to live lives of confidence, we had better
get hold of the truth that God has called and invested us
with a grace identity. We too are the servants of God.

We often call ourselves names. Useless. Inconsistent. Weak.
God calls us names too. Salt. Light. Overcomers. Chosen.
Justified. Royal. Beloved. Friends of His. Children of the Father.

These are more than precious thoughts, pretty bouquets from
a sentimental God. They form the backbone of our confidence.
Sadly, we frequently forget who we are and become, as Michael
Griffiths would put it, like 'Cinderella with amnesia',[1] the bride
who doesn't remember her name or to whom she is betrothed.

Identity amnesia brings weakness and creeping
paralysis. The God of Covenant found a bunch of
half-starved Hebrew slaves who were being treated
like scum by their Egyptian oppressors, and decided
to remind them of their real name: 'Chosen'.

Within a few weeks they forgot their new name and
dubbed themselves with a lesser title, 'grasshoppers':
'we felt like grasshoppers, and that's what they
[our enemies] thought, too' (Num. 13:33).

If their choice of name seems ridiculous, then remember
that there are many Christians today who feel it's very
spiritual to denigrate themselves 'for God's glory'.

As a group, evangelical Christians consistently rate lowest
in the self-esteem polls. If we're not careful, we can become
Christianised versions of the man in Jean-Paul Sartre's *The Flies*
who cries out: 'I stink! Oh, how I stink! I am a mass of rottenness...
I have sinned a thousand times... and I reek to heaven.'[2]

Of course there is someone who is more than willing
to help with our little renaming ceremonies: Satan is
the enemy of identity. 'This is my Son, whom I love,'

shouts the Father from heaven as Jesus allows John
to push him under the water – identity affirmed.

'If you're the Son of God, do some magic tricks,' whispers the
devil a couple of weeks later – identity questioned and denied.

So much is accusation a part of the satanic personality that his
very name 'devil' comes from a root word meaning 'to accuse'.
Satan shouts loudly too – the Greek word for accuser means
'one who speaks before a public tribunal'. No wonder so many
Christians seem to drag themselves along the pathway of faith,
weighed down with guilt and self-doubt. An expert lawyer for
the prosecution (who has been in the business for quite a while,
and knows all the tricks) is on their case. John Newton prayed:

> *Be Thou my shield and hiding place*
> *That, sheltered near Thy side,*
> *I may my fierce accuser face,*
> *And tell him Thou hast died.*[3]

Our identity is rooted not in our accomplishments, our success, our family history, or the opinions of others. It is rooted in what God has done in Christ, and who He has made us in Christ.

Unlike us, Elijah couldn't look back to a crucified,
resurrected Jesus of history, and find his 'grace identity'
there – but he knew that the hand of God was upon him.
So, without apology, he stood before the king and queen.

And so Elijah strode into the royal courts, and fired his
prophetic missile, which was greeted by stunned silence.

The royal servants would have known better than to speak;
they just stood there, frozen by the moment, their own
breathing loud in their ears. Even the courtiers, Ahab's
advisors and friends, were stunned into silence, fearful
of the king's face. His eyes were cloudy, his face drained
of blood, and he was staring at the ground. After a few
seconds that seemed like hours, Ahab looked up, his eyes
clear now, sharp with anger, darting around the crowd.

And then they realised. The little man
from the country was gone.

–   –   –   –   –

His story can seem a long way from ours.

Let's face it, most of us will never stand before princes or kings.

Announcing words of judgment won't be part of our portfolio.

And taking control of the weather won't be on
our agenda, although the ability to produce a
consistent English summer would be helpful.

So what has the story of the Tishbite who stood
before the king have to do with us?

Surely it all comes down to this: faith is a call to courageous living.

It's what nudges us to disagree with that racist comment
at work, to stand alongside the underdog that nobody
else likes, to refuse to give our ear to the gossip that's
virally spreading through the church we attend.

It's what makes the difference when the doctor
delivers a grim-faced diagnosis, or we wake in the

middle of the night sweating with fear, the shadows
of our bedroom seemingly filled with menace.

We mustn't just associate courage with the epic, with the stand-
off, with the Luther King 'I have a dream' moments, with the
brave soul who leaps to the rescue, ignoring personal threat.

Courage is often a quiet hum rather than a momentary roar.

The determination to believe when we feel
hemmed in with question marks.

The choice to trust when that pain in our
body just keeps getting worse.

The faithfulness to remain when it would be easier to give up.

Courage.

It's a characteristic of the noble, to do what is right
in the face of whatever threat might come.

For Elijah, it means standing in the intimidating
grandeur of the royal court.

For us, the scene might be far less dramatic.

But for those who follow Christ, courage will be
needed, whenever we live, and wherever we live.

---

[1] Michael Griffiths, *Cinderella with Amnesia: Practical Discussion of the Relevance of the Church* (London: IVP, 1975)

[2] Jean-Paul Sartre, *No Exit and Three Older Plays* (New York: Random House/Vintage Books, 1948), p77

[3] Taken from the hymn *Approach, My Soul, the Mercy Seat* by John Newton (1779)

Three:
SHAPED FOR SIGNIFICANCE

'Then the LORD said to Elijah, "Go to the east and hide by Kerith Brook, near where it enters the Jordan River. Drink from the brook and eat what the ravens bring you, for I have commanded them to bring you food."

So Elijah did as the LORD told him and camped beside Kerith Brook, east of the Jordan. The ravens brought him bread and meat each morning and evening, and he drank from the brook. But after a while the brook dried up, for there was no rainfall anywhere in the land.' – 1 Kings 17:2-7

FAITH FOR ALL SEASONS

He was determined not to run.

To run would undermine the statement; it would give
the impression that his confidence in God had only been
a momentary thing – a suicidal outburst at best.

But now that the job was done, it seemed like the adrenalin that
had been pumping around his body was draining swiftly, and
as he hurried away, merging into the crowd now, he realised
that he hadn't the faintest idea what he should do next. There
had been no arrest, no sharp order barked at the royal guards
to roughly haul him off to the cells. There had been... nothing.

So now what?

It wasn't that he searched hard and long for the answer. God
took the initiative, because the word of the Lord came to
Elijah. As he trotted along as fast as decorum and expediency
would allow, he suddenly recognised that voice he had come
to trust, so much so that he had risked his life to obey its
commands, gently but clearly spoken over the months.

Perhaps what he sensed he heard seemed quite ridiculous.

Surely now was the time for Elijah to tour the nation,
repeating the prophetic word of judgment to all who
would listen. Or perhaps he should stay in Samaria
and make himself available, just in case the king
decided to respond to God's word and repent.

But the voice was firm, insistent: 'Leave here.'

Quickly he came to the edge of the city and turned eastward.

-      -   -   -   -

Perhaps we all dream of a day when a phone call will come
that summons us to a delicious opportunity – a dream job,

an expanded ministry opportunity, an opening to serve in a context that offers possibility, potential and greater impact.

I remember the day that call came. Having planted a church in the UK, one that had grown to a reasonable size with its own building, I took the call from one of the leaders at our denominational headquarters. It was the equivalent of a head-hunting enquiry, an offer that was hard to resist, at least for this enthusiastic (and ambitious) 29-year-old.

I was being asked to go and work alongside the leader of one of Britain's largest churches. The inference was that, in time, due to the ongoing ill-health of the current senior leader, I was being groomed to take the senior leadership of this thriving congregation.

I was thrilled, not only by the confidence that was being expressed in me, but by the potential of the appointment. It would be inappropriate to divulge further details, but this seemed to be a door that God was opening.

We're like that, aren't we?

We assume that the promotion, the greater responsibility, the bigger salary, the more influential platform – that it *must* be His will for us to step up, step out, advance and progress steadily up the ladder. Our language is peppered with words that betray our love of what is bigger or greater.

Kay and I prayed a lot about the decision, not least because there was a fly in the ointment. We had already been invited to take a role in a church in Oregon.

In terms of 'promotion' (a word that I'm hesitant to use in terms of ministry), progression it was not. I'd been a senior pastor for seven years, albeit of a relatively small congregation. Now I would be an associate.

Financially, we would be paid less. Not only was this a challenge, but a few of my friends assumed that we we're being lured by cash to America, when in fact the opposite was true.

Our shiny just one-year-old car, a gift presented to us by our current congregation, would be traded in for an ancient gas-guzzler that cost us £600, and in which we would have to drive across America.

We owned a house. Now we would need to sell it, with little profit, and move into rented accommodation.

But through a strategic second phone call that came two agonising weeks after the first, we felt we heard God tell us to say no to the sparkling opportunity, and head for relative obscurity, and an opportunity for us to grow in faith and trust in what, at times, felt like a wilderness.

Elijah went east. We, in our own tiny little test of obedience, headed west.

And it was one of the best steps we ever took.

-　　-　　-　　-　　-

God has a keen sense of irony.

Elijah prophesied a lengthy drought, and then God spoke again and sent him off to a place called Kerith. There's double irony here, in that Kerith was a brook, and brooks are quick to dry up. A river would have been a more logical choice.

And then, the name 'Kerith' means 'drought'.

Elijah prophesied drought and so was now headed towards... drought.

What was God up to?

Elijah was suddenly snatched off stage almost as soon as he had made his first dramatic entrance, and was destined to be parked by the brook for a long time.

Why?

Was it just that Elijah needed to hide away from Jezebel's roving assassins?

After all, to be a prophet of Yahweh was to invite execution, and a number of the prophets had gone into hiding as a result. Previously we saw that a man called Obadiah had helped protect a whole guild of prophets.

As the chief steward of Ahab's palace, Obadiah enjoyed a place of prominence, more like a Prime Minister than a butler. (An ancient seal has been found with the words, 'To Obadiah, servant of the king' written on it, and some scholars think it refers to the same man.)

He was a highly placed mole, a spy for God, who was indeed 'servant of the king', but (as the name Obadiah declares in the Hebrew) he was the 'servant of Yahweh' too.

This brave, faithful man had worshipped the true God since his youth, and now he personally undertook a rescue mission for the prophets - hiding 100 of them in two caves, providing food and water for them from the palace stocks. (Ahab and Jezebel were unwittingly feeding the prophets of Baal and Yahweh at the same time.)

So perhaps we might assume that God was providing a hiding place for Elijah until Jezebel's temper cooled, particularly as the English translation of 1 Kings 17 includes the word 'hide'.

But our assumption would be wrong. Elijah was never called to hide in the conventional sense of the word. Indeed, when Jezebel issued a personal death threat sometime later in Elijah's life, and the prophet took things into his own hands and ran away, God sent him straight back into the situation. No, the *safety* of Elijah wasn't the primary motivation for the trip to Kerith - the *shaping* of Elijah was.

Even though Elijah had responded with commendable faithfulness and obedience to his first mission, there was still a great deal of shaping and further preparation needed before he could stand on Mount Carmel and take on the prophets of Baal. One success didn't mean that graduation day had arrived.

Greatness, as the Bible defines it, never comes suddenly.

It is normally forged in the furnace of time.

It has been said that before Moses could lead the Hebrews out of Egypt, he had to spend 40 years in Pharaoh's palace learning to be a somebody, then 40 years as a man on the run learning to be a nobody, and then the last 40 years leading the people of God, discovering that God uses nobodies.

King David spent a lot of his early days watching sheep - hardly the most exciting lifestyle.

But the Good Shepherd was at work, continually investing in David's character during those long hot days and cold nights, preparing him for the greatness that was to come.

Peter had to navigate confusion, disappointment, failure, and sit by the fire with Jesus before he could preach his first sermon or discover the healing power of God pulsating from his own shadow.

The reason for the shaping process is simple. God is more interested in the character of His children than He is in their gifting.

So even though Elijah was flushed with success, it was nevertheless school time for him, and the junior school was called Kerith. It gave Elijah a tough education.

Forget any ideas of the exiled prophet sitting by a beautiful, crystal-clear stream, enjoying fabulous scenery and having a party with his Maker – another day in paradise as the water bubbled and sang. Kerith was an ugly place, where a small seep of water had worn away rock and stone to gouge out a stark, deep gash in the desert. And the water would have been muddy and murky and dotted with debris.

The weather was searing – often 49°C in the afternoon – which would have helped the growth of thick, green algae on the surface of the brook. Far from being rested in an idyllic resort, Elijah was holed up in the back end of the desert and forced to sip scum soup in order to survive.

Why?

For one thing, Elijah had to live out his message.

He had *spoken* God's judgment – now he had to flesh it out with prophetic action. When God told the prophet, 'Hide yourself,' He used a term that would be more accurately translated as 'absent yourself'. The same Hebrew word is used in Genesis 31:49: 'May the LORD keep watch between you and me when we *are away from each other*' (NIV, my emphasis).

Once again, we see that God didn't call Elijah to run away. Rather, his exit was a dramatic sign of God's displeasure, an acted-out shout from Yahweh. Prophecy is more than words. Some of the most powerful prophetic moments I have ever witnessed have been dramatic.

A hammer methodically tapping a bottle.

A person lifted into the air, held up by their friends.

Jeremiah threw pots around.

Ezekiel made scale models of cities and then lay on
his side for about thirteen months (and then rolled
over to the other side for another six weeks).

Micah took all his clothes off and went around naked to prove
a prophetic point (a style that I'm certainly not promoting).

And Agabus, a leading prophet in the Early Church, prophesied
Paul's forthcoming imprisonment by tying him up with a belt.

Actions speak louder than words.

This, however, was more than an act of drama: Elijah
was being called to live with the implications of his own
message, even though it cost him dearly. Admittedly, God
sent him to a familiar place, for Tishbe was on the Kerith,
and so it was most likely Elijah's youthful stomping ground.
He would have played in this area as a child. But there was
still a cost, because now he had to live outside the warmth
of the community of family and friends, alone with God.

He had spoken the word. Now he had to live the word. The
challenge to us is obvious: as Christians we must continually
ensure that we are living by truth as well as believing it, lest
we fall into 'believism' – the idea that intellectual adherence
to a body of truth is sufficient. James warns us about being
deceived by the idea that *hearing* the word is enough
(James 1:22), and all Christians, particularly preachers, need to
know that to *preach and proclaim* the word is not enough either.

Ted Engstrom's words sting: 'It's dishonest to talk about
the power of prayer and lead a prayerless life. Isn't it
dishonest to talk about forgiveness and fail to forgive?'[1]

Living the message starts with the so-called small issues.
We may not be guilty of armed robbery, but are we paying

our bills on time? An appointment with a prostitute may be a million miles from our thinking, but what do we watch on TV late at night, when we've worked hard and 'just need to relax...'?

Bill Hybels is the well-known, dynamic leader of the huge Willow Creek Community Church near Chicago. He has known great success in ministry, but has also been willing to admit that he and his team have made mistakes, especially in the realm of discipleship.

And not only is Hybels humble, but he pays close attention to details:

> One evening, I stopped by the church just to encourage those who were rehearsing there for the Spring Musical. I didn't intend to stay long so I parked my car next to the entrance. After a few minutes I ran back to my car and drove home.
>
> The next morning I found a note in my office mail box. It read: 'A small thing, but Tuesday night when you came to rehearsal you parked in the 'No Parking' area. A reaction from one of my crew (who did not recognise you after you got out of your car) was, "There's another jerk in the 'No Parking' area." We try hard not to allow people – even workers – to park anywhere other than the parking lot. I would appreciate your co-operation too.' It was signed by a member of our maintenance staff.
>
> This man's stock went up in my book because he had the courage to write to me about what could have been a slippage in my character. And he was right on the mark. As I drove up that night I had thought, 'I shouldn't park here, but after all, I am the Pastor.' That translates 'I am an exception to the rules.' But that employee wouldn't allow me to sneak down the road labelled 'I am an exception.' I am not the exception to Church rules or any of God's rules. As a leader I am not an exception: I'm to be the

*example. According to scripture I am to live in such a way
that I can say 'Follow me. Park where I park. Live as I live.'*[2]

And living the message in daily obedience means
that we know what we are called to do – and
what we are not called and gifted to do.

Elijah was called to what seemed to be a quick retirement.
After all, one national prophecy in three years is hardly
a heavy caseload. But at this period of his life, his
arena of operation was the delivery of just one single-
sentence sermon. He could have travelled as an itinerant
revivalist, but that wasn't his mission at that point.

He could have joined the prophetic school, brought some
leadership to that group, and taken care of them – but that
was Obadiah's task, and not part of Elijah's job description at
this time, although he would get involved with schools later.

Like Elijah, we need to have a sober, rational
assessment of our gifting, so that while we do develop
and grow, we don't step out way beyond it.

Of course, spheres are flexible; they expand and change, and
sometimes God completely changes our sphere of operation,
so we shouldn't get too locked up in them. However, an
understanding of our sphere helps us to respond appropriately
to opportunities that come our way. There are some things
that I know I should never do – singing, for example. I used
to sing in a Christian rock band, but all aspirations in that
direction ended because I became increasingly aware that
when I sang people cried out to God – and not in repentance.

'The best way to create a good, healthy self-image
is to be honest about self-definition. I would like
to sing, but I can't.' I'm with Steve Brown.[3]

I also know there are some things that are not part of my *primary* calling, which I may nevertheless occasionally give myself to. When you are clear about your calling, you can rejoice at the successes of others and avoid feelings of jealousy or insecurity, because you know that you are secure in what you do, and that God has called others to function differently.

One word of warning about spheres: we shouldn't use this kind of talk as an excuse to avoid doing the things that we all find tedious. 'I can't stack the chairs or pick up a piece of litter after the meeting, because it's not my calling.' We do well to remember that we never leave the sphere of servanthood, whatever our arena of operation.

–   –   –   –   –

And so the God who is full of surprises called Elijah to the silent surprise of isolation.

And the Lord made all the catering arrangements for Elijah, but his methods were unusual – he was to be fed twice each day by a flock of ravens.

Some commentators rebel at the idea of God commanding a squadron of birds to feed a prophet: one says that the word for 'ravens' (*haorebim*) is similar to the word for 'Arabs' (*haarabim*), so therefore it was Bedouins who fed the exiled Elijah, rather than birds.

However, I agree with the commentators who say that the Bedouin idea removes from the miraculousness of the event and doesn't have any foundation in the biblical account. It seems clear to me that God directly provided for Elijah.

But don't be tempted to romanticise the scene – grinning birds landing in perfect formation, each dropping their piece of sirloin steak onto a silver platter marked with an 'X' in the middle like a helicopter pad, as Elijah tucks his napkin into his collar and picks up his knife and fork...

Of course, there were practical reasons for God hiring a bunch of bird-caterers. While we've already established that Elijah wasn't hiding in the conventional sense of the word, nonetheless there still might have been the odd bounty hunter out looking to make a fast shekel out of presenting Elijah's head to Ahab and Jezebel. If Obadiah (or perhaps one of God's seven thousand faithful still living in Israel) had been given the catering contract, they might have been followed by a would-be hitman. But birds are impossible to follow – and besides, what suspicion would be stirred by the sight of a bunch of ravens flying by with food in their beaks? Quite apart from the issue of security, the provision from the ravens must have been a source of encouragement to the lonely prophet-in-exile.

Twice a day he was reminded that God was supernaturally involved in every detail of his life.

But perhaps there was another reason for this bizarre arrangement.

Elijah obviously had to learn that God is full of variety and surprise.

Passionate believers fall quickly into the trap of legalism, so it was time for Elijah to learn that God was no sterile, do-things-by-the-book-type deity. Thus Elijah ends up with a bird as a maître d'.

He probably groaned at the thought – the possibility of being drip-fed from a bird beak wasn't exciting. Ravens feed on offal, carrion and general rotting matter – they love to hang around rubbish tips. And now those very same beaks were under divine orders.

And weren't ravens designated as unclean according to the Law? Elijah may have frantically searched his memory. What was it the Law said? 'These are the birds you are to detest and not eat because they are unclean: the eagle, the vulture, the black vulture, the red kite, any kind of black kite, *any kind of raven*' (Lev. 11:13-15, NIV, my emphasis).

Technically, the Law wasn't being broken, because Elijah wasn't eating the birds; they were just playing waiter. But even so, what was God up to? Yahweh was teaching his servant that he will not be locked in by preconceived ideas or legalistic straightjackets.

When it comes to the things that God wants to do, the past is often the enemy of the present - especially if God's blessing was evident in methods used in the past.

Why is it that the radicals who historically rode the crest of God's blessing in the past are so often the opponents of the next wave of His blessing? The answer can be summed up in one word: inflexibility. We get focused on the *style* in which God moved and the methods that He blessed yesterday. We then get suspicious when, because God is moving on and is the author of freshness and creativity, He decides to do something utterly new that shatters all of our preconceived ideas.

There were to be lots of surprising twists and turns ahead as Elijah followed God, and the flying food force helped the prophet prepare for the unexpected - though I doubt whether Elijah realised that when he was woken up each morning by a large flock of ravens spitting their offerings at his feet.

And then, every day after the birds left, there was just Elijah - and the stillness.

—   —   —   —   —

It was such a sudden transformation.

One moment he was standing in the presence of the king of the land; the next he was breakfasting with winged scavengers.

The day before he'd squeezed through the bustling crowds of the city, senses stirred by the noises and the smells of a relative metropolis; now there was only the relentless but gentle bubbling of the brook.

There had been no time to be swung up onto the shoulders of Yahweh's faithful as a new folk hero who had taken on the king himself. No pats on the back, no warm smiles and well dones.

Just water.

Those birds again.

And God.

Perhaps it's hard for us in our frantic, addicted-to-activity society to relate to this scene. Most of us feel that the urgent jangling of the alarm clock is really like a starter's pistol to the beginning of every hurried day. The moment our feet hit the floor they land on a fast-moving conveyor belt – things to do, places to go, people to see, life in the fast lane, busy, busy...

Our smart phones demand our instant response. We live fragmented lives; multi-tasking, texting, interacting on social media, glued to our handsets.

Even our leisure has a frantic feel about it. Theme parks provide us with the latest stomach-churning 'happening'. We don't want to relax. We want to see, touch, feel everything.

Turn on the TV. Rent a DVD, or stream a movie. Binge watch a TV series. Save planet Earth from certain destruction in the privacy of your front room via your computer or console game...

It's been said that we are a FOMO generation.

Fear of missing out.

We have to respond to that text or email. It might be important.

We have to check Facebook. Who knows?

Someone may have posted a photograph of
the cheese sandwich they ate for lunch.

We don't want to miss that.

And so stillness becomes something to avoid.

Silence is perceived as our enemy. The jogger out in
the beautiful countryside plugs his brain into music.
Never mind the hum of nature and the sound of the
breeze in the long grass, give me other sounds...

Phone the doctor. You're on hold, but don't worry
– we'll play you music, lest you should have to
endure twenty seconds or so of... silence.

Applaud the person who works a seven-day week (90 hours,
or so they say), who works out in order to maintain efficiency,
who listens to subliminal teaching about increasing
productivity while he sleeps... and who dies of a heart
attack at the age of 43, slumped in the arms of the wife
whom he didn't get to know that well... there wasn't time.

And then we stop just long enough to ask a man who goes
by the name Prince of Peace to take charge of our lives.

But on we race, keep up the pace, pound the treadmill.
Not much has changed, only now we add to our
busyness a catalogue of church-related activities.
Or perhaps we don't. There just isn't time.

The gentle murmuring of the brook seems a million miles
away from where we're at in the twenty-first century.
'It's all right for you, Elijah, but life's not like that now.'

And, in many ways, that's true. The idea of dropping out for a while remains an elusive dream for most of us.

So what are we to do?

After all, stillness must be a priority. In the original Hebrew, when God directs Elijah to Kerith there is a strong emphasis that says: 'I'll meet your needs, Elijah – but I'll meet them there.' Kerith was non-negotiable.

Perhaps we can begin by learning to build stillness in the midst of busyness. You can't get away from it all for a month or maybe even two days – but you can for ten minutes.

Leave a book – maybe a novel that you enjoy – in the bathroom so that you can take a five-minute vacation when you visit the smallest room. (Be careful that you don't park there for hours because you got too engrossed in the book – this will not bless the other members of your household.)

Ignore the crowded lift and climb the stairs.

Remember the television comes fitted with an off button.

Write a few scriptures on a piece of paper, stick it on the fridge, and stop once in a while to read and think about them.

Deliberately slow down. I do a great deal of travelling, and my tendency is to work out just exactly how long it will take me to get to a place, and then go screaming down the motorway with foot pushed hard on the accelerator.

Breathless but triumphant, I arrive having shaved a whole ten minutes off my previous landspeed record. This great feat was accomplished by my refusing to stop for petrol. To do so would have wasted a precious five minutes. The downside of this decision is that I've been driving perilously close to empty. Thus most of the trip has been spent with my back arched with tension over the steering wheel and my eyes darting towards the petrol gauge every 17 seconds, as I quickly overtake in order to save another few moments.

The other night, however, I tried my Kerith experiment.

I left half an hour earlier for my speaking engagement, and took the country lanes rather than the motorway. I decided to take my time, enjoy the scenery and chat with God. I'm sorry to report that no land speed records were broken – but I arrived at my destination relaxed, refreshed and raring to go. Strange as it may seem, you can install a brook into your car.

I have some friends in America who are passionate about astronomy. Apparently their best star-gazing experiences take place when they pack their equipment into their car and drive a few miles out of town. They have to get away from the upward glare of the city lights in order to focus on what's above. Of course, the stars are always there – it's just that the fluorescent glare of the streets shrouds them from view.

God is there, but often He is made distant by the glare of our feverish living.

Stillness allows us to turn down the lights and zoom in on Him for a while.

Perhaps, like me, you'd like a real Mount Carmel type of faith: mighty miracles, bold confidence, fearless faith. The story of Elijah shows us that there is a road to Carmel.

It passes through Kerith.

[1] Ted Engstrom, *Integrity* (Waco, TX: Word, 1987), p92

[2] Bill Hybels, *But I'm an Exception* (*Leadership Magazine* Spring 1988, vol 9, no 2), p37

[3] Steven Brown, *Don't Let Them Sit on You* (Eastbourne: Kingsway, 1988)

Four:
ZAREPHATH

"Then the LORD said to Elijah, "Go and live in the village of Zarephath, near the city of Sidon. I have instructed a widow there to feed you."

So he went to Zarephath. As he arrived at the gates of the village, he saw a widow gathering sticks, and he asked her, "Would you please bring me a little water in a cup?" As she was going to get it, he called to her, "Bring me a bite of bread, too."

But she said, "I swear by the LORD your God that I don't have a single piece of bread in the house. And I have only a handful of flour left in the jar and a little cooking oil in the bottom of the jug. I was just gathering a few sticks to cook this last meal, and then my son and I will die."

But Elijah said to her, "Don't be afraid! Go ahead and do just what you've said, but make a little bread for me first. Then use what's left to prepare a meal for yourself and your son. For this is what the LORD, the God of Israel, says: There will always be flour and olive oil left in your containers until the time when the LORD sends rain and the crops grow again!"

So she did as Elijah said, and she and Elijah and her family continued to eat for many days. There was always enough flour and olive oil left in the containers, just as the LORD had promised through Elijah.

Some time later the woman's son became sick. He grew worse and worse, and finally he died. Then she said to Elijah, "O man of God, what have you done to me? Have you come here to point out my sins and kill my son?"

But Elijah replied, "Give me your son." And he took the child's body from her arms, carried him up the stairs to the room where he was staying, and laid the body on his bed. Then Elijah cried out to the LORD, "O LORD my God, why have you brought tragedy to this widow who has opened her home to me, causing her son to die?"

And he stretched himself out over the child three times and cried out to the LORD, "O LORD my God, please let this child's life return to him." The LORD heard Elijah's prayer, and the life of the child returned, and he revived! Then Elijah brought him down from the upper room and gave him to his mother. "Look!" he said. "Your son is alive!"

Then the woman told Elijah, "Now I know for sure that you are a man of God, and that the LORD truly speaks through you."'
– 1 Kings 17:8-24

'God's man or woman is early selected
and slowly educated for the job.'[1]

Elijah had been about a year by the brook now,
but he had learned a lifetime's lessons.

Perhaps, initially, curiosity had nibbled away at
him: what was going on in the big city?

Had there been a change of heart from the king –
or was Elijah now Israel's most wanted man?

But as the weeks went by, the questions diminished as the encouraging voice seemed to boom in the Kerith silence. One thing was beyond doubt – God was taking care of him; the clockwork arrival of the ravens seven hundred times over assured him of that.

God has no graduates in His university. The process of learning and shaping is continuous, and from a human perspective, God seems to be in no hurry. Kosuke Koyama writes in *The Three Mile an Hour God* that God works at the speed a person walks – and we may well find His pace painstakingly slow. Koyama uses the 'Wilderness College course' in which the Hebrews were 'enrolled' as an example: 'Forty years for one lesson. How slow, and how patient. No university can run on this basis... God goes slowly in His educational process of humans. Forty years in the wilderness points to his basic educational policy.'[2]

It was time for the next stage in the prophet's development: he was commanded to break the brook-side camp and head for Zarephath.

But there were plenty of very good reasons why it was the last place to go.

First of all, it was in the opposite direction from Samaria; now he would be further away from the action. It was about eighty miles away – a hefty trek.

More significant was it that Zarephath was in a foreign country – and just eight miles down the coast from Jezebel's home city of Tyre.

A real danger zone.

Then, to top it all, the man who had been supernaturally provided for twice a day would from now have to rely on the charity of an impoverished widow – who was most likely not a follower of Yahweh. It may have seemed like an ironic joke on God's part, for in a time of scorching drought, God sends him from Kerith ('drought') to Zarephath ('smelting furnace'). While wishing to avoid lame analogies about refining fire, God turning the temperature up and all that, I think you'll agree that there is a certain irony in it all, as Elijah trudges eighty sunbaked miles to a divinely appointed oven.

Who says the road to greatness and glory is easy?

-     -   -   -   -

Hunger had gouged her face deeply; stark hollows where cheeks should have been, sucked in now by malnutrition.

Her skin, once smooth and lovely, had been folded deep with creases by the sharp edge of poverty.

Her hair hung lank over bony shoulders, and her arms and legs were pathetic spindles, impossibly fragile.

But it was her eyes that told the story.

They were cold and bleak; she was a dead woman walking. Life had been nothing more than a day-to-day fight for existence for as long as she could remember. With her husband long gone, she had been left to fend for herself, and now even her son was too weak to do the basic chores. As she scurried around by the city gates, perhaps she remembered better days, when her husband gossiped and laughed there with the other men of the city, their voices echoing around the walls as darkness closed in at the end of the day.

But that was all a very long time ago.

Now there was nothing left, and no chance of better days.

For some while she had felt some vague hope; a persistent thought had been nagging at her mind for weeks:

'A man comes'.

A man comes.

From God.

It was probably just wishful thinking – or maybe a premonition about the angel of death, coming for her and her bag-of-bones son. It was time to let hope die, and life with it. One last meal then, and afterwards perhaps the gods would be merciful and let them die in their sleep...

Perhaps he caught sight of her as he sat by the city gate, exhausted by the five-day journey, wondering what to do next. He would have felt the agony that was written all over her, maybe even wavered for a moment about that prayer for drought cried out so long ago. In a way, even though the thought was perverse, he was partially responsible for her pain. He watched her scrabbling around for a few sticks to make an evening fire, conscious of that nervous gnawing that comes from being a stranger in a foreign land.

And then he realised.

It was her.

Put yourself in Elijah's sandals for a few moments. You're tired, hungry, and probably desperate for some human company after a year in isolation. Warmly assured that God has got everything organised, you've emigrated, though there is some concern as you are now in pagan territory that is mainly inhabited by Baal worshippers.

You're looking forward to your first meal provided by human hands in over twelve months – and you discover that God's provision is a very confused and undernourished woman with a death wish.

Perhaps Elijah looked around the city square and noticed some other more well-to-do ladies with a good deal more flesh on their bones and hope in their hearts.

Why couldn't it be one of them whom he was to stay with?

If I had been in his position, I would have been tempted to look elsewhere, especially when God had said, 'I have commanded a widow to sustain you.' And then, when Elijah asks for food, she says that she doesn't have enough and that this is her funeral meal anyway.

With a slight cough of embarrassment, I would have heartily apologised for my stupid error of mistaken identity and, with a sigh of relief, beaten a very hasty retreat.

But not Elijah.

The circumstances seem to contradict what God has said. They often do.

It takes the greatest grace to live in the gap between a promise that God has given and the fulfilment of that promise. Some of the most amazing heroes that I have ever met have spent decades in that seemingly barren territory. Unknown, and often uncelebrated, they continue to trust, refusing to loosen their grip on God.

'I'm providing for you at Zarephath,' says God, and Elijah finds himself staring at abject poverty and death – hardly a comforting confirmation.

But something else begins to ring in his mind as
the woman describes her empty bowl and jar.

Prophets are often triggered by the sight of objects
which seem to suggest a divine truth.

Like a prophetic litany, a repetitive chant,
words begin to form in Elijah's mind.

A prophetic rap from God.

Quickly Elijah assures the woman that all will be well, and
asks her to prepare a meal. The black and white portrait
then begins to burst into colour as a miracle blossoms.
For 'many days' the food is miraculously provided. The
supernatural has restored laughter and hope to a widow's
home once again, and Baal gets a slap in the face too.

An ancient stele has been found portraying Baal holding
a spear which contains a plant or a tree. One of his many
names was 'Baal ben Dagan' (Son of Dagan), and 'dagan'
means corn. This particular Baal was therefore supposed
to be a vegetation god, whose blessing was needed for
plentiful corn. Many scholars believe that it was Baal ben
Dagan that was the principal deity in Sidon. And now Elijah
multiplies the corn - but he does so in the name of Yahweh.

Zarephath was a place of strategically significant miracles - true
signs and wonders, supernatural acts that declared truth - and
furthermore, for Elijah, school was very much back in session.

And one of those lessons is often overlooked.

As we zoom in on a tenuous, fragile domestic
situation, we discover this challenging truth:

What we are at home and in close
relationships is what we really are.

Elijah emerged from the enforced solitude of Kerith with many life lessons learned, but now he has to learn to live out those discoveries in the rough and tumble of a family life.

Archbishop William Temple said, 'Your religion is what you do with your solitude.' While there is a measure of truth in that statement, it isn't the whole truth. I find it easy to be massively spiritual when I'm alone. I really enjoy going out to pray on the glorious South Downs. It's easy to be very holy while walking along with the warm sunshine on my back, quietly singing or praying or thinking about Scripture. For me, 'religion' in solitude is the easy part. The difficulty is working all that wonderful spirituality out at home, especially in past days when our children were young. Now I remember them with more than affection – in fact, I'd give anything to go back to those days. But when walking through them, life wasn't always easy, as every parent knows.

Dirty nappies to change. Violin practices at 7am. The need to change the TV channel from the movie you're engrossed in, so that your children can catch up with the antics of their favourite duck.

I'm certainly humbled by Catherine Bramwell-Booth's description of her Salvation Army father, Bramwell Booth:

> When he told us about Christ, told us who He was and what He did, we understood. We felt... that our Father himself was like the Christ he loved.[3]

I'm grateful that I'm not alone in being humbled and challenged to do better in the domestic cauldron of family life. Prominent American politician and leading Christian, Senator Mark Hatfield, confesses: 'The home is the toughest environment of all for leaders. Why is it that the ones we love the most are the ones that we are most impatient with?

My wife has often said to me, "I wish you were as patient with your children as you are with your constituents."[4]

Of course, it's not only leaders who are prone to suffer from this split-personality spirituality. Tony Campolo wisely counsels young people:

> Sometimes, after Christian young people have been off to a church camp or religious weekend retreat, they come home 'talking the language of Zion' and, with pious platitudes, give testimonies of how their lives have been changed by God. However, none of this has any significance unless it changes the way they act at home. Those who have had genuine conversion experiences will give evidence of their new life in Christ by how they relate to their parents.[5]

Let us not be fooled into believing that our public behaviour represents who and what we really are – in that arena there exists all kinds of artificial constraints of propriety and performance.

We are truly what we are in the home.

The real us is to be most accurately measured by the jokes we tell when we're with our 'let our hair down' friends, rather than the Sunday morning persona that fellow churchgoers see each week.

It's in the home that bruising words can so easily tumble out of our mouths.

It's in the home where we can misunderstand, and be misunderstood.

And it's in the home where the pressures of life can nudge us into taking out our frustration on those who are closest to us.

Elijah was about to discover what that felt like.

—   —   —   —   —

It's amazing how human beings have such short memories when it comes to God's blessing – and limited loyalty too. Israel marches across the dry ground that seconds earlier was the Red Sea. They celebrate with great excitement – and then very shortly after they start moaning and pining for Egypt.

The Hebrews displayed the remarkable
human tendency that we all share.

We quickly forget what we should remember,
and remember what we should forget.

This amnesia is also in evidence at the trial of the Lord Jesus. Hearts that had swelled with the word 'Hosanna!' on Palm Sunday quickly switched tack and screamed, 'Crucify Him!' The religion barons who fuelled the crowd's fury only succeeded in whipping them into a bloodthirsty frenzy because of this human tendency to quickly forget the handiwork of God.

And now Elijah becomes a victim of this syndrome.

For months he is the honoured and welcome guest
in the widow's home – the man whom God sent,
the agent of deliverance, the hero of the hour.

But today's hero quickly becomes tomorrow's
scapegoat when things go wrong.

In the midst of a miracle, death comes as the widow's son falls sick and finally passes away. Suddenly, it's all Elijah's fault. Elijah represents Yahweh, so when the widow feels frustrated and angry with God, God's prophet gets it in the neck: 'What do you have against me, man of God? Did you come to remind me of my sin and kill my son?'

One moment Elijah is the man of the year, the next he's a murderer. Notice the widow seems quickly to connect the death of her boy with something evil that was in her past (though we don't know the details, she obviously had a skeleton or two hanging in her cupboard), but in her grief, she blasts Elijah with three unjustified bullets. The temptation for Elijah must have been to justify himself.

'You've got something against me.' ('What do you mean, lady? I've been happily living here and we've lived in an amazing, unfolding miracle of provision every day.')

'You've reminded me of my sin.' ('I didn't say a word.')

'You've killed my son.' ('I didn't do it – he's been sick for a long time, as you well know. I've been praying for him, and now what do I get?')

But despite the spite, Elijah ignores the false accusation (and the bad theology) that declared, 'This has happened because I've done wrong.'

This wasn't the time for personal defence or theological debate – the boy had stopped breathing, and Elijah had come to love this family. Now he learns to pray, not because of anger at national occultism or righteous indignation – but because he cares.

Blazing passion for the law drove him to pray the drought prayer; sobbing compassion for the grieving drives him to raise the dead.

And driven he is. He certainly has a no-holds-barred approach to the calamity. Boiling anger and frustration are hurled at God Himself:

> Then Elijah cried out to the LORD, 'O LORD my God, why have you brought tragedy to this widow who has opened her home to me, causing her son to die?'
>
> (1 Kings 17:20)

This is no passive speech.

This is a crying heart opened to heaven – a rage, even – that spills like a torrent as Elijah looks at the whitening, cold corpse on his bed.

And then he 'stretched himself' upon the boy, not once, but three times. How does a fully grown man 'stretch' his limbs out on the small body of a child? Elijah literally covered the child's body with his own. Some commentators suggest that he did so as if to say to God: 'Let my life be his life, my breath be his breath. Take me rather than him.'

As he did so, yet another taboo bit the dust – the one about touching dead bodies: 'All those who touch a dead human body will be ceremonially unclean for seven days' (Num. 19:11).

The Jews regarded a corpse as exceptionally defiling – that's why the graves or sepulchres were 'whitened' so that they would be easily recognisable and so avoided.

But Elijah was prepared to go to any length to bring resurrection, including making himself personally 'unclean'.

It was the same kind of compassion that caused Jesus to touch the dead body of another widow's son hundreds of years later.

Compassion must be at the heart of any cry for the miraculous. God has no interest in providing Holy Spirit ignited fireworks for the delight and entertainment of the Christian public. He offers His power because He cares for people – and lest we be guilty of becoming like the sign-seekers who followed Jesus around, we need to ensure that our motive is the same in everything we do for God. Evangelism without compassion is heartless expansionism.

And in this traumatic time, Elijah was kind.

-　　　-　　　-　　　-　　　-

The story has a happy-ever-after ending.

A beautiful reunion takes place as Elijah carries the now-living child downstairs and announces: "'Look!' he said. 'Your son is alive!'" Notice there's not even a hint of self-praise in Elijah's words; no sense of, 'Wow! Look what happened when *I* prayed.' But the woman knows it is Elijah whom God has heard, and so is able to exclaim, 'Now I know for sure that you are a man of God, and that the LORD truly speaks through you.' When Elijah and the widow first met, she referred to 'the LORD *your* God' – she was prepared to acknowledge His existence, but had no personal experience of Him.

Now that's all changed, for she has seen truth, and that truth has been modelled in Elijah.

Those who rub shoulders with the property of God – the people of God, who belong to Him – run the risk of being changed for ever.

Paul Borthwick tells the story of missionary Gordon Maxwell:

> *He went to India as a missionary, and his Christian conduct and commitment were evident to all. On one occasion, he asked a Hindu man to teach him the local language. The Hindu man replied, 'No, sahib, for you will convert me to Christianity.' Maxwell tried to clarify: 'You don't understand, all I want you to do is teach me*

the language.' But the Hindu replied, 'I will not, for no one can live with you and not become a Christian.'[6]

We are called to *be* good news, not just talk about it.

That's why we're called salt and light, for both of these elements change and affect. Both disturb the status quo by their very existence and presence.

Such knowledge should cause us to be careful, for as J.R. Miller says:

> *There have been meetings of only a moment which have left impressions for life, for eternity. No one can understand that mysterious thing we call influence... yet... every one of us continually exerts influence, either to heal, to bless, to leave marks of beauty; or to wound, to hurt, to poison, to stain other lives.*[7]

To live with Elijah was to discover that the God of Israel was lodging there too. And with that reality in place, Elijah came to the end of that school session.

He had spent time in solitude, and discovered a million truths about God and himself there.

He'd lived those truths out in the challenging context of friendship and family.

It had been a long and rigorous training course, and had demanded everything he had.

In his poem *The Ladder of St Augustine* Henry Wadsworth Longfellow speaks the truth about greatness of character:

> *The heights by great men reached and kept*
> *Were not attained by sudden flight,*
> *But they, while their companions slept,*
> *Were toiling upward in the night.*

But while the education process had been tough, both Kerith and Zarephath were gentle hillsides compared with the mountain that Elijah was now called to climb.

That mountain was called Carmel.

[1] Soren Kierkegaard, *Attack Upon Christendom* (Princeton, NJ: Princeton University Press, 1968), p195

[2] Kosuke Koyama, *The Three Mile an Hour God* (London: SCM, 1979), pp3,6-7

[3] Catherine Bramwell-Booth, *Commissioner Catherine* (London: Darton, Longman and Todd, 1983), p77

[4] Harold Myra (ed), *Leaders* (Carol Stream, IL: CTI Word, 1987), pp52-53

[5] Tony Campolo, *Seven Deadly Sins* (Wheaton, IL: Victor Books, 1987), p57

[6] Paul Borthwick, *Leading the Way* (Milton Keynes: Authentic media, 2003), p66

[7] J.R. Miller, *The Building of Character* (Whitefish. MT: Kessinger Publishing, 2007)

Five:
CARMEL

'Later on, in the third year of the drought, the LORD said to Elijah, "Go and present yourself to King Ahab. Tell him that I will soon send rain!" So Elijah went to appear before Ahab.

Meanwhile, the famine had become very severe in Samaria. So Ahab summoned Obadiah, who was in charge of the palace. (Obadiah was a devoted follower of the LORD. Once when Jezebel had tried to kill all the LORD's prophets, Obadiah had hidden 100 of them in two caves. He put fifty prophets in each cave and supplied them with food and water.) Ahab said to Obadiah, "We must check every spring and valley in the land to see if we can find enough grass to save at least some of my horses and mules." So they divided the land between them. Ahab went one way by himself, and Obadiah went another way by himself.

As Obadiah was walking along, he suddenly saw Elijah coming toward him. Obadiah recognized him at once and bowed low to the ground before him. "Is it really you, my lord Elijah?" he asked.

"Yes, it is," Elijah replied. "Now go and tell your master, 'Elijah is here.'"

"Oh, sir," Obadiah protested, "what harm have I done to you that you are sending me to my death at the hands of Ahab? For I swear by the LORD your God that the king has searched every nation and kingdom on earth from end to end to find you. And each time he was told, 'Elijah isn't here,' King Ahab forced the king of that nation to swear to the truth of his claim. And now you say, 'Go and tell your master, "Elijah is here."' But as soon as I leave you, the Spirit of the LORD will carry you away to who knows where. When Ahab comes and cannot find you, he will kill me. Yet I have been a true servant of the LORD all my life. Has no one told you, my Lord, about the time when Jezebel was trying to kill the LORD's prophets? I hid 100 of them in two caves and supplied them with food and water. And now you say, 'Go and tell your master, "Elijah is here."' Sir, if I do that, Ahab will certainly kill me."

But Elijah said, "I swear by the LORD Almighty, in whose presence I stand, that I will present myself to Ahab this very day."

So Obadiah went to tell Ahab that Elijah had come, and Ahab went out to meet Elijah. When Ahab saw him, he exclaimed, "So, is it really you, you troublemaker of Israel?"

"I have made no trouble for Israel," Elijah replied. "You and your family are the troublemakers, for you have refused to obey the commands of the LORD and have worshiped the images of Baal instead. Now summon all Israel to join me at Mount Carmel, along with the 450 prophets of Baal and the 400 prophets of Asherah who are supported by Jezebel."

So Ahab summoned all the people of Israel and the prophets to Mount Carmel. Then Elijah stood in front of them and said, "How much longer will you waver, hobbling between two opinions? If the LORD is God, follow him! But if Baal is God, then follow him!" But the people were completely silent.

Then Elijah said to them, "I am the only prophet of the LORD who is left, but Baal has 450 prophets. Now bring two bulls. The prophets of Baal may choose whichever one they wish and cut it into pieces and lay it on the wood of their altar, but without setting fire to it.

I will prepare the other bull and lay it on the wood on the altar, but not set fire to it. Then call on the name of your god, and I will call on the name of the LORD. The god who answers by setting fire to the wood is the true God!" And all the people agreed.

Then Elijah said to the prophets of Baal, "You go first, for there are many of you. Choose one of the bulls, and prepare it and call on the name of your god. But do not set fire to the wood."

So they prepared one of the bulls and placed it on the altar. Then they called on the name of Baal from morning until noontime, shouting, "O Baal, answer us!" But there was no reply of any kind. Then they danced, hobbling around the altar they had made.

About noontime Elijah began mocking them. "You'll have to shout louder," he scoffed, "for surely he is a god! Perhaps he is daydreaming, or is relieving himself. Or maybe he is away on a trip, or is asleep and needs to be wakened!"

So they shouted louder, and following their normal custom, they cut themselves with knives and swords until the blood gushed out. They raved all afternoon until the time of the evening sacrifice, but still there was no sound, no reply, no response.

Then Elijah called to the people, "Come over here!" They all crowded around him as he repaired the altar of the LORD that had been torn down. He took twelve stones, one to represent each of the tribes of Israel, and he used the stones to rebuild the altar in the name of the LORD. Then he dug a trench around the altar large enough to hold about three gallons. He piled wood on the altar, cut the bull into pieces, and laid the pieces on the wood.

Then he said, "Fill four large jars with water, and pour the water over the offering and the wood."

After they had done this, he said, "Do the same thing again!" And when they were finished, he said, "Now do it a third time!" So they did as he said, and the water ran around the altar and even filled the trench.

At the usual time for offering the evening sacrifice, Elijah the prophet walked up to the altar and prayed, "O LORD, God of Abraham, Isaac, and Jacob, prove today that you are God in Israel and that I am your servant. Prove that I have done all this at your command. O LORD, answer me! Answer me so these people will know that you, O LORD, are God and that you have brought them back to yourself."

Immediately the fire of the LORD flashed down from heaven and burned up the young bull, the wood, the stones, and the dust. It even licked up all the water in the trench! And when all the people saw it, they fell face down on the ground and cried out, "The LORD—he is God! Yes, the LORD is God!"

Then Elijah commanded, "Seize all the prophets of Baal. Don't let a single one escape!" So the people seized them all, and Elijah took them down to the Kishon Valley and killed them there.

Then Elijah said to Ahab, "Go get something to eat and drink, for I hear a mighty rainstorm coming!"

So Ahab went to eat and drink. But Elijah climbed to the top of Mount Carmel and bowed low to the ground and prayed with his face between his knees.

Then he said to his servant, "Go and look out toward the sea."

The servant went and looked, then returned to Elijah and said, "I didn't see anything."

Seven times Elijah told him to go and look. Finally the seventh time, his servant told him, "I saw a little cloud about the size of a man's hand rising from the sea."

Then Elijah shouted, "Hurry to Ahab and tell him, 'Climb into your chariot and go back home. If you don't hurry, the rain will stop you!'"

And soon the sky was black with clouds. A heavy wind brought a terrific rainstorm, and Ahab left quickly for Jezreel. Then the LORD gave special strength to Elijah. He tucked his cloak into his belt and ran ahead of Ahab's chariot all the way to the entrance of Jezreel.'
– 1 Kings 18:1-46

In Samaria, the man they called king
sat alone, silent, thoughtful.

The room in which he sat was splendid.

Every wall was breathtaking, panelled from floor to ceiling with intricately carved ivory; figures of lions, griffins and sphinxes stared down. The place overflowed with the trappings of royalty. Even the bed ends, table tops and chair backs were ivory-clad.

But Ahab had no eyes for such things now.

His servants had been dismissed, scurrying away at his terrible yell, bowing and retreating at the same time. His dark moods were common enough, but the household never ceased to be terrified of them. The palace was on edge. Sometimes the king would shut himself away for days on end, and the servants knew well that to disturb him was to die.

With the door shut, he was alone with his thoughts – and fears.

How could it have come to this? Here he was, the king of Israel, a man who had known fabulous wealth and massive power. He had lived a life that other men could only dream about, with a sumptuous palace, beautifully decorated, no expense spared, a country house in Jezreel, and anything his heart desired.

The word of his command was backed up by about two thousand chariots and ten thousand men – the royal stables at Megiddo had been a pride and joy since Solomon's time. He had chosen to base himself in a fortified city that would provide the highest security confidence: Samaria was set on a hill about three-hundred-feet high. It was surrounded by two fortification walls – the outer wall around nineteen-feet thick, the inner wall five-feet thick.

Good fortune had kissed his friends as well: Israel's upper classes had enjoyed long, luxurious years of prosperity. Of course, the peasant classes had suffered in order to pay for the few to live in luxury. Extortion and oppression were rife, but what of it? The poor were nothing – little people, expendable.

Perhaps it was meant to be that way – the will of the gods?

The thought that the poor were victims by destiny had brought a smile to his face and his twisted heart. There was no need for concern or conscience. It was meant to be.

However, despite all that had been, the drought was now taking its toll. He'd heard about the scorched farms, brown and barren. Stories were circulating about the growing numbers of corpses that were to be seen lying in the fields, some crawling with corruption, others bleached white bones, poor pickings for the birds.

Samaria, the royal city, was suffering the worst effects of the drought. It was as if Yahweh had targeted him, singled him out for punishment. Fine treatment for a man who had named his children in Yahweh's honour!

Now his horses were dying. His servants would always find water for the palace, but over at Megiddo Stables they had encountered real problems with their supply, and now reports were coming in that those once beautiful, sleek animals were dropping like flies. So desperate had he been that he, the king, had taken his steward Obadiah out into the countryside on a secret mission to try to find grazing pasture, but the mission had been a failure.

Kicking his footstool aside, the king got up and walked to the window. How often the view from there had brought him pleasure. Looking eastward, he could see the rich hills of Gilead on the horizon.

Gilead was the home of that pious troublemaker, Elijah. Four years earlier, no one in the land had ever heard that cursed man's name. Back then he was just another worthless peasant, garbed in his crude camel skins.

But now the common people were saying that it was Elijah who was really in charge of. Israel: the wretched man had announced famine, and then disappeared out of sight. He hadn't been seen or heard of for years. Ambassadors had been sent out to all the surrounding nations, demanding that Elijah be extradited if he was living within their borders. Threats, pleas, bribes – nothing had worked.

Then, at Jezebel's suggestion, the last few remaining Yahweh prophets had been arrested and tortured in the hope that they would provide some information. However, despite the unspeakable things that had been done to their bodies, none had talked. In the end, Jezebel had suggested that they all be put to death. After all, when the master of the lower chamber had finished with them, they were almost dead anyway, so why not just be rid of them and their irritating rantings for good?

Yet none of this had led to the discovery and arrest of Elijah. Perhaps, Ahab hoped, the obnoxious man was dead. Perhaps one of those whitened skeletons was all that was left of the man.

He smiled at the thought.

Suddenly, his moment of pleasure was shattered by a nervous tapping at the door.

Hadn't he left strict orders? Furious, he spun around from the window, spat out an obscenity and marched towards the door. Someone would suffer for this interruption.

The door opened, and Obadiah quickly bowed.

'News, your Majesty. It's the Tishbite. He's back –
I spoke with him today. Sir... he wants to see you.'

Ahab punched the air with rage; his teeth grinding with
frustration, death in his eyes. He, the king, was being
summoned by a fugitive peasant. The indignity.

The audacity.

He looked back at Obadiah, who quickly bowed his
head, the perfect servant now, awaiting instructions.

–   –   –   –   –

The dry, cracked trail exploded with dust as the king
and his mounted bodyguards drew their horses to a
halt. The king was in a hurry. The Septuagint (Greek
translation of the Old Testament) version of 1 Kings
says that he 'ran out' in eagerness to meet and confront
the man who had haunted his dreams these last few
years: the most wanted man in the whole of Israel.

'So there you are, troublemaker!' snarled Ahab, his mouth
twisted with rage. The Hebrew word for 'troubler' is a
very strong insult, meaning 'one who brings disaster'.

Elijah looked back at his enemy and decided not to disguise
the feelings of contempt that boiled within him. He knew
that this was a dangerous moment. With one swiftly barked
order, the king could have one of his guards run the prophet
through. The torture chamber was another possibility, to
'encourage' Elijah to reverse the drought-curse. But God
had said, 'Show yourself to the king.' Elijah spoke out:

> *I have not made trouble for Israel... But you and
> your father's family have. You have abandoned the
> LORD's commands and have followed the Baals.*

*Now summon the people from all over Israel to meet
me on Mount Carmel. And bring the four hundred
and fifty prophets of Baal and the four hundred
prophets of Asherah, who eat at Jezebel's table.*

(1 Kings 18:18-19, NIV)

Ahab opened his mouth to protest. After all, *he* was in charge
around here, *he* gave the orders, and here was this religious
fanatic upstart telling him what to do and where to go.

It was outrageous.

But no words came, and he was surprised to find himself
just nodding meekly. The sergeant of the guard was
flabbergasted. His hand sat ready on his sword, just
waiting for the order to strike and silence the cursed
prophet for good. But no order came and, without
another word, Elijah turned and walked away.

\-   \-   \-   \-   \-

It was early morning, but already the sun was high upon
Carmel, giving a rippled, shimmering appearance to the
crowds that were climbing the hillside. It had been like
this for a few days now. It must have taken some time for
the people to travel from all over Israel. By the thousand
they came, many of them gaunt and thin, weakened
by the drought years, struggling to the summit.

They knew better than to disobey the royal decree: the
king had ordered that every able-bodied person gather at
Carmel, and only the fools or the dying ignored the king
– with the notable exception, of course, of Queen Jezebel.
She hadn't come this far by obeying or respecting her
husband, and she wasn't about to start. She stayed away,
and her 400 Asherah priests stayed away too, by order of
their royal patron. The 450 Baal priests were in attendance,

and happy to be there. Carmel had become a favourite site for the evening feasts. This, they thought, was their home territory. They felt safe and secure on the mountainside.

The crowds were so thick that some fought over vantage spots. They knew that it would take hours, days even, for everyone to arrive. The rich would have taken the prime spots, jockeying to be closer to the temporary shelter which had been erected to protect the king from the scorching sun. The poor would have been unable to see a thing, probably relegated to the Kishon lowlands and kept informed by the rumours and conversations passed slowly down the hillside. Elijah was nowhere to be seen. He was most likely in one of the 2,000 caves that litter Carmel – a warrior preparing for the battle of his life.

Only when the king, his bodyguard and a huge entourage arrived did the crowd begin to talk about some action taking place. At this stage, all they knew was that the king had called them all together, and that the Gileadite Elijah was involved in the meeting as well. They waited, joked, speculated, renewed old friendships, exchanged the latest family news, showed off sons and daughters with pride...

Carmel was an ideal location for the showdown between God and Baal.

The mountain was always a lush green, as it was the first to catch the sea rains as the clouds marched towards the east. Of course, the Baal prophets would have been delighted by this, as Carmel would have been the one place in Israel that would show little evidence of the drought. Perhaps the people would forget the drought judgment for a while, and consolidate their commitment to their new gods.

Carmel, however, was to be the scene of a cosmic courtroom drama, with geographical witnesses for the prosecution in the case of Yahweh versus Baal.

To the north rose the snow-capped triple peaks of Mount Hermon. The mountain itself was a stark reminder to everyone, for here children had been sacrificed by fire to the Baals since the time of the Judges. It was a grim monument that spoke of a thousand dark nights of orgies, apostasy and the murder of innocents.

To the west lay the clear blue waters of the Mediterranean.

The sails of Tyrian trade ships could be seen here and there, a reminder to all of the trading alliance that had been entered into with Tyre – that treaty that had caused so much trouble. Sailing ships that spoke of greed and ungodly alliances; disastrous dealing.

Then down at the foot of Carmel, beyond the Kishon River, was the royal country house of Jezreel and the huge Baal temple that stood next to it.

A royal palace that housed an idolater king and a witch queen.

The witnesses gave silent testimony.

Finally came the hour when the crowds craned their necks, pointed their fingers excitedly down the hillside and muttered their speculations behind cupped hands, because the Gileadite was spotted walking steadily upwards. As he walked, he thrust the end of his staff onto the parched earth with each step – a man in the rhythm of resolve.

Elijah was coming.
The court was in session.

There is something eerie about the silence that can suddenly fall upon a huge crowd. One moment it is a teeming mass, pulsating with laughter, gossip, irritation, questions, opinions, a million mingled words. Then it seems as if every mouth closes, every ear strains to listen, unwilling to miss a thing - the crowd now was a murmuring giant stilled.

I imagine that such a silence fell upon the huge Carmel gathering that day so long ago, as Elijah climbed up onto a rock, waited for the last voice to be still, and laid down the gauntlet of challenge.

'How much longer will you waver, hobbling between two opinions? If the LORD is God, follow him! But if Baal is God, then follow him!'

With just two sentences, Elijah brilliantly argues his case.

God's case against His people.

Point one: worshipping both God and Baal is spiritually and intellectually debilitating. To try to do so is to waver or, more accurately, 'limp on two crutches' or 'stagger'. Some experts in the Hebrew language say that the word used here describes a bird that is walking along a tree branch and suddenly discovers that it splits into two.

Instead of making a choice, it puts one claw on each branch, and tries to continue its journey, accomplishing nothing but the splits in the process.

Another translator renders this: 'How long will you walk lame on both knee joints?'

The whole episode reveals that Elijah possessed a sharp, sometimes cutting and sarcastic sense of humour. Thus Elijah graphically demonstrates the pathetic foolishness of religious syncretism - 'mongrel religion', as one writer puts it.

'How long?' asks Elijah.

Point two: Elijah connects with a memory buried deep in the hearts of the Israelites as he describes the Lord as 'Jehovah'. This was the name by which the Lord God had been known to the people ever since their forefathers came out from the land of Egypt. It stirred memories of the covenant God of Abraham, Isaac and Jacob.

Elijah is aiming for high stakes here: he wants to see a national renewal of covenant. Just as Samuel called the people to recommit themselves to Jehovah at the coronation of King Saul, so Elijah is looking for a new pledge of allegiance after no less than 400 years of darkness and backsliding.

Point three: make your choice.

God will not foist Himself upon human beings, but respects the will of a person to choose whom he will serve. Elijah's Hebrew words literally mean, 'If Yahweh is God, go after him; but if Baal, go after him.'

But the unearthly hush remained on the crowd. Perhaps the common people were nervous of offending the king – or unsure about the response of the Baal prophets.

Whatever the reason, their silence discredited them, for they had all experienced a supernatural drought that had been initiated by a servant of Yahweh.

That should have been enough to convince them who was really God. But doubt and rebellion are stubborn partners when they have lived too long in the human heart. It was time for the real God to stand up.

In human terms, it must have appeared that the odds were stacked heavily in favour of the Baal prophets. It's good for morale to have 450 of your like-minded friends around when you're involved in an important contest – you can encourage and spur one another on as mutual cheerleaders.

Elijah stood alone.

There's no record of the prophets in exile being on hand to help, and Obadiah the double agent is keeping his customary low profile. No wonder Elijah later exaggerated: 'I'm the only one of the Lord's prophets left.'

He let the Baal priests pick which bull they would use for the sacrifice – and then let them go first in the fire-summoning contest. But then again, none of this made the slightest bit of difference, because they were singing their songs to a fake god. It was a serenade to nothingness.

They went on for about eight solid hours.

They danced until they were fit to drop – limbs aching, muscles searing with hot pain, driven on through normal thresholds of exhaustion by a frantic sense of despair.

Interestingly, the Bible uses the word 'halt' or 'stagger' to describe their dancing. It is the same word that Elijah used in his 'How long will you *stagger* between two opinions?' speech. Ironically, the height of the Baal frenzy included a dramatisation of the staggering that Elijah had described so powerfully earlier in the day. They shouted and screamed and sang until they were hoarse; until their feeble voices faded to a whisper:

'Oh Baal, hear us...' The Hebrew writer of 1 Kings allows them no sense of dignity, delivering three hammer-blow phrases of indictment:

> *But there was no response, no one*
> *answered, no one paid attention.*

(18:29, NIV)

For the first hour or two the crowd was probably rapt with attention. Then, like all crowds when there's no action and little hope of anything much developing, boredom sets in.

Unrelated conversations start.

The children go back to their chasing games,
and the moment of tension is past.

Enter Elijah the comedian, eager to spice up the occasion with a few witty asides. One thing is sure: months and months alone with God haven't dulled his keen sense of ironic humour. In fact, while this sweaty praying is going on, Elijah is having a party. That wicked sarcasm emerges again, as he offers the exhausted idolaters some homespun advice on how to wake a god up.

'Shout louder,' he encourages. 'Maybe he's
deep in thought... maybe he's asleep.'

This was another one of Elijah's many 'in' jokes – Baal Melqart was believed to be a vegetation deity who had to be awakened each spring from his winter hibernation; thus the need for all the stamping and yelling.[1]

Evidently Baal needed a wake-up call.

Then the Hebrew text reveals Elijah at his earthy, outrageous best: 'Maybe he is going to the toilet'. (The translators of the NIV Bible obviously couldn't cope with such a blunt, crude character, so they've tidied the text up by having Elijah say, 'Maybe he's travelling.')

The Baal priests responded to Elijah's snide
comments by yelling louder.

Nothing.

There was still no response.

It was time for them to bring out their final weapon. Taking up swords and spears, they stabbed and gouged themselves until the whole area was awash with blood. Perhaps it was designed to be a hint to the apparently stupid Baals: *'Look, gods, we need fire. Bright, colourful, red stuff like this.'*

One commentator suggests that this was a solemn act of blood-bonding between worshippers and the devil they worshipped; a bloody covenant of desperation. But it was in vain.

Eight agonising hours later, the chopped limbs of the bull-sacrifice sat, dried crisp by the sun, but with no sign of the slightest spark.

By now, the sacrifice would have been a mass of flies, all eager to gorge themselves on the blood and offal, turning the Baal altar into a seething putrefying mess. This itself was testimony to the obscenity that was Baalism.

But there had been no pyrotechnical response from the heavens.

The truth was out.

Baal was no god at all.

The people had been deceived. Many of them had sacrificed their own children – and all for a lie.

The natural response from the crowd would have been one of stunned anger. Fists clenched into a knuckle-white ball, and angry words yelled that vengeance would be taken. Perhaps mothers wept as they remembered their newborns, and replayed the horrifying images of the sacrifice of their little ones.

In their darker moments, in the middle of hot, sleepless nights, they'd tossed and turned and tried to remember

what their babies had looked like, and then, when
the image of the tiny face came, they'd tried to erase
it lest they be driven over the brink of madness.

And in those sweating, breathless moments,
they'd told themselves that the pain was worth it
because it was for the gods – a noble offering.

But it had all been for nothing, the slaying of their darlings for
idols that couldn't hear or see, for a god that had never been.

Tears of anger, recrimination, guilt and rage flowed freely.

And just when it may have seemed like there was no
comfort – nothing that could possibly make life worth living
again – the Gileadite cupped his hands to his mouth:

'People! Come here to me.' No need for them to stand at a
distance, for this was to be a totally genuine miracle. Let
the people come as close as they liked. Truth can stand the
most intense scrutiny. No second invitation was needed.
The people ran to him – a great, sad, curious mass.

The old altar was in disarray, broken down by neglect
and vandalism. Or had the destruction been the sour
fruit of the Baal feasts that happened here on countless
nights: a ceremonial desecration of the old Yahweh
altar; another spit in the face of the living God?

Carefully, Elijah picked up 12 stones, and as he wedged
them together to form a new altar, he began to speak
out the tribal names of Israel: 'Reuben, Simeon, Levi,
Issachar, Zebulun, Dan, Naphtali, Gad, Asher, Joseph...'

Then came the revolutionary revelation: the last two stones,
and the accompanying words, 'Judah and Benjamin.' The crowd

drew breath, and then quickly began to mutter, staggered by the prophet's act. He was suggesting that the southern kingdom, arch enemies now of Israel, should be included in one united nation under God. But before the political chattering could continue, Elijah called for a shovel, and began to dig a trench.

The true worker of miracles doesn't need to whip a crowd into a frenzy of expectation.

Cleverly constructed hype or crass showmanship accompanied by emotion-wrenching music isn't required in order to see the impossible.

Slowly, methodically, Elijah dug, pausing every now and then to wipe the sweat that beaded his brow and stained the back and armpits of his rough shirt. It was hard work, and he grunted as his body jarred each time the spade hit the hard-baked earth, but it was a necessary labour, because Elijah wanted every living soul to see that the real God needed no help, no conjuring tricks or sleight of hand.

This was going to be a 100% bona fide miracle.

Elijah took some of the wood and placed it on the altar, and then put the cut bull, carefully blooded and quartered, upon the wood. Fourteen litres of water were brought from the Kishon, and they poured it over everything on the altar, filling the trench.

By sacrificing an ox, he made a powerful statement, and we mustn't miss the significance of it. Elijah could have called for a lamb, or a pair of doves, or a kid goat for the sacrifice.

But he insisted on an ox.

Why?

According to the Law, whenever a priest or prophet wanted to make atonement for the sins of himself and his own immediate household only, he would offer an ox. It was a private act, rather than an offering on behalf of the people.

> *Aaron is to offer the bull for his own sin offering to*
> *make atonement for himself and his household*
>
> (Lev. 16:6, NIV)

So why an ox, when Elijah could have made an offering on behalf of the whole nation on Carmel? The answer is probably simple: quite apart from the fact that Elijah wanted to be totally clean before God himself, he had absolutely no right to make an offering on behalf of a people who had not repented for themselves. Such an offering would have been a mockery; a lifeless ceremony, void of meaning or purpose.

Until the people themselves decided to engage their will and change their minds, no ceremony would have any merit. So he took an ox, because he, and he alone, wanted to be right before Yahweh. We must never forget that God refuses to overrule a person's will. There is a sense of sovereignty about the will of a human being.

Next, Elijah invited representatives of the people to soak the sacrifice in yet more water: a total of twelve jars full; one for each tribe. The whole altar area was a soggy mess and the ditches were thoroughly waterlogged.

Why the water routine? Elijah wanted the people to know that when the fire came, it really did come from God.

Yahweh didn't need a hand or (unlike Baal) a hint.

We'll do well to remember this when we are tempted to exaggerate or embellish ever-so-slightly a testimony of what God has done. There is no glory in a lie – even a well-intentioned lie.

Go on, Elijah. Fill the buckets again. Splash that fire-drowning water all over the place.

The real God needs no help.

At last, all was ready. The crowd quietened, that unearthly silence again. Thousands – from the nervous, agitated Ahab resplendent in his fabulous robes to the lowliest beggars – stared at Elijah. He seemed to be waiting for something, his hands on his hips, looking up at the sky, towards the sun. Perhaps some wondered if he was looking for the rays of the sun to focus on the soaked altar, but his faith wasn't in solar heat. He was just waiting for the sun to climb to that place in the sky that announced that it was, in modern terms, three o'clock in the afternoon – the time that God had decreed for the afternoon sacrifice in the Temple at Jerusalem. The people glanced frequently at the Yahweh altar. No flies spotted this sacrifice; it was kept pure, and the sharpness of the salt repelled the insects. At last, satisfied that the moment had come, he lifted his hands and began to pray, calmly but deliberately.

-       -   -   -   -

It had been done before – by David, the friend of God. He had built an altar to God 200 years earlier, when he made the classic and oft-quoted statement, 'I will not offer to God that which costs me nothing.' God always responds to costly obedience. Fire fell from heaven and consumed David's burnt offering – a swift, dynamic gesture of divine approval.

But Elijah was inspired by more than historical precedent.

This was more than a gamble.

God had spoken very specifically to Elijah – that much is revealed by a prayer that stirred up a sense of ancient destiny: 'O LORD, God of Abraham, Isaac and Jacob, prove today that you are God in Israel and… that *I have done all this at your command*' (1 Kings 18:36, my emphasis).

It was also an ideal way to strike at the evil Baal myth. For just as Baal's lordship over corn was refuted by a miracle at Zarephath, and Elijah's cutting jokes portrayed Baal as the god who needed to be yelled at in order to wake him up, so Baal was also supposed to be the god of fire.

In fact, it was believed that the house where Baal lived was made and tested by fire.

Consider another one of those ancient inscriptions written thousands of years ago about Baal and the house that a personality called Kothar-wa-Khasis was supposed to have built for him. It throws light on this idea:

> *Fire is set on the house, flame on the palace,*
> *Behold a day and a second, fire eats into the house*
> *Flame into the palace, a third, a fourth day,*
> *Fire eats into the house, flame into the palace.*
> *A fifth, a sixth day, fire eats into the house.*
> *Flame, in the midst of the palace,*
> *Behold on the seventh day,*
> *The fire departs from the house,*
> *the flame from the palace.*
> *Silver turns from blocks, gold is turned from bricks.*

The popular myth was that Baal was literally at home with fire. But the flames were not destined to come from that non-existent palace furnace in the sky, but from the hand of the true God, Yahweh.

Was there a moment when nothing happened?

A few seconds that would have felt like minutes to the crowd, now on tiptoe? We'll never know, but we do know that Elijah continued to speak to God. It was a brief, succinct prayer. No time spent rambling around in word circles, trying to stir faith; no 'vain repetitions' here. 'O LORD, answer me! Answer me so these people will know that you, O LORD, are God *and that you have brought them back to yourself*' (1 Kings 18:37, my emphasis).

Delay or not, the final words of the prophet's prayer were significant and provided the trigger for the power of God. It was when Elijah stated the need for the nation to repent and turn back to God that the miracle was ignited. No wonder he was the forerunner of John the Baptist. God has no interest in providing cosmic firework displays for the sake of thrilling interested spectators. Signs and wonders are purposeful – designed to elicit response from rebellious human hearts.

–   –   –   –   –

It all took just five stunning seconds, but it would be the subject of countless conversations around evening camp fires for centuries.

The little children who, at the moment of impact and ignition, had been snatched and clutched close by fearful mothers, would remember that terrible fire for the rest of their lives, and would thrill their own grandchildren as they recalled the event.

The day that they saw the hand of God.

It was shocking in its suddenness, and in its awesome power.

It came from no cloud, for in drought-stricken Israel the sun rode high and unchallenged in a clear blue sky.

This was not lightning.

It was not a spontaneous ignition from within the
sacrifice itself, some cleverly provoked combustion,
for they saw the fire flash from the heavens, blinding
white hot as it seared through the still afternoon air and
smothered the altar in a second, evaporating the water
and leaving only hissing, sizzling charcoal where the
wood and the bull had been just a moment before.

Perhaps the crowd stood impossibly still and quiet
for ten or fifteen seconds, their minds struggling to
catch up with what their eyes had just witnessed.

Just one solitary voice began to cry out, choking with
tears, 'The LORD – he is God! The LORD – he is God!'

And then a nation fell on its face, and it pushed itself
as low as it could into the baked earth. The solo
became the anthem of thousands, as in unison Israel
made the spontaneous declaration of truth – a great
roar of what appeared to be genuine repentance and
faith: 'The LORD – he is God! Yes, the LORD is God!'

Astute commentators have observed that
their cry did not include a personal pronoun:
'The LORD, he is *our* God,' or '*my* God'.

Perhaps Elijah would recall that lack of
personal commitment later.

Who knows what Ahab did in those historic moments? Did he
remain solidly on his throne, an angry sneer smearing his face?
Or did he do the politically expedient thing and join in with
the shouting? We can be sure that among the thousands, there
were 450 who refused to join in – a silent, unyielding protest.
The prophets of Baal had no song to sing, no cheer to offer. And
after a while, as inevitably the cries of worship subsided and

the people slowly began to climb to their feet, all eyes were turned on the men who had led a whole nation into deception.

They had shattered families and brought about the drought-judgment because of their despicable wickedness. The verdict was clear: the prophets of Baal were guilty. Time for justice and, according to the Law that had been ignored for so long, only one sentence could be passed on an idolater. It was time for death.

The people were quick to obey when Elijah ordered the arrest of the bruised and bleeding Baal prophets. Ignoring their cries and demonic curses, they dragged them all – arms pinioned – down through the thick Carmel undergrowth to the Valley of Kishon. By the low waters of the river, where Judge Barak had triumphed over the Syrians years earlier, they ran them through with the sword.

In the lengthening shadows of the late afternoon, the swords flashed again and again. The condemned most likely died as they had lived: crying out to gods Melqart and Asherah, even then refusing to believe that they had sold their lives for an empty lie. The Kishon River reddened, flowing back as it did towards Phoenicia – bad blood going home. A mass grave was probably hastily dug, and the bodies thrown in without ceremony. The place became known as Tell-el-Kass: the priests' mound.

–　　　–　　　–　　　–　　　–

The first edition of this book was published a decade before the internet became part of our lives. Instant access to world news, including terrible atrocities, was not available back then. In the years that have followed, we have been blessed with instant communication, and cursed with the capacity to view terrible images that are uploaded by those who wish to terrorise us. Images of knife-wielding extremists standing before black flags; their helpless, traumatised victims kneeling before them, dressed in orange, are now part of our consciousness.

I remember and regret the day when an email arrived with a link to a video of a now infamous ISIS killing, when a caged man was burnt to death. Not paying proper attention, I clicked on the link.

I admit with shame, I couldn't look away.

I wish I had.

And so now I cannot just rush on when I read about the slaughter of 450 people, killed with the sword in the name of God.

Was it right for Elijah to engage in this mass slaughter?

As we've seen, these Baal prophets had committed horrendous crimes; countless children had died horrible deaths because of their evil influence. Perhaps this was judgment for the babies who would never grow up – little lives snuffed out by the fire; for the mothers who would be crippled by guilt and grief until their dying day; for the young men and women who had lost their innocence for ever, recruited to serve as temple prostitutes, condemned to lurk in the 'sacred' groves for years, ready to embrace the next sweating stranger.

To let them live would risk more of the same. Was this a cancer that just had to be cut out of the nation, the death of a few to save many? Perhaps.

Or perhaps it was a natural overflow of anger from people who had been mortally wounded by these evil sorcerers.

Perhaps it was justice.

Or maybe you and I can't really grasp what was going on here, because we look at the terrible mass execution through eyes that can't see and understand the culture of the day. This was a battlefield. Was it a just response to the atrocities committed by the Baal priests?

Perhaps.

But I still have to be honest and say that, in an ISIS-infected world, my stomach turns at what Elijah apparently commanded.

I don't like it.

Surely we're not supposed to celebrate anyone's death, whatever their crimes.

I can be honest about my revulsion.

God isn't nervous or angry because I don't like it.

And perhaps that's enough said for now.

—   —   —   —   —

The people were called to choose: Baal or the Lord.

Decisiveness comes from faith. It's the usual fruit.

After a shared meal with Jesus, little Zacchaeus (I always think of him as being like Danny DeVito up in a tree) immediately makes a life-altering choice to make financial restitution to the many he had defrauded – a hugely expensive decision.

The two on the road to Emmaus have supper with the resurrected Jesus, and then, having realised who their guest is, they immediately head back along the road to Jerusalem – a dangerous trek through shadows that often hid bandits,

because the cosmos-shaking news had been broken to
them during the breaking of bread: Christ is risen.

Cue action.

A few weeks ago, I saw faith birth immediate action.

Closing out a sermon at Timberline Church in Colorado, my
home church, I invited the congregation to sing the beautiful
song *Here's My Heart, Lord*. I added that this could be an
opportunity for some who were not currently followers
of Jesus to sing their way into the kingdom. Rather than
praying a prayer, they could sing their invitation to Jesus to
take control of their future, to forgive their past, to cause the
miracle of rebirth, regeneration by the Spirit, to happen to
them. I added that I felt that in the coming hours and days
some would come to me to tell me that this had indeed
happened to them – that they had sung their way to Jesus.

The service ended, and a lady approached
me in the foyer, handing me a card.

It simply said:

12.29. ☺

What did this mean – a number and a smiley face?

She clarified her scribble.

'It happened at 12.29pm today, Jeff. I sang my
way to Jesus. I decided!' Her face was beaming.
And then she invited me to turn over the card.

It read:

Next Saturday. Baptism.

The moment she chose to follow Jesus, she decided to go public with the decision. And so, in the chilly waters of a Colorado lake, she was baptised in water.

She chose faith. And she chose obedience, immediately.

–   –   –   –   –

It had been a full day – the fullest day of Elijah's life.

He had battled with gargantuan pressures and overthrown the forces of darkness. He had been taxed to the very limit of his psychological resources.

He must have been exhausted – and if ever a human could have been tempted to say, 'Enough is enough. I've done my part,' it was Elijah.

He could have been forgiven, perhaps, for wanting to linger on the lower slopes to shake 10,000 hands and receive as many words of warm congratulations, for he was a hero now.

But the work wasn't finished yet.

Elijah walked up to the very summit of Carmel, conscious that the sky was still a flaming, shimmering sheet of brass. As ever, it was time to pray again. A boy or young man joined him, simply described in Scripture as 'his servant'. We can't be sure about the identity of this person. Legend has it that he may have been the widow's son from Zarephath, dedicated to serving the man whom God had used to deliver him from death. He may have been a volunteer from the crowd, eager to bless the man who asked God for fire.

It may have been Elisha in the first faltering steps of ministry.

As they climbed, the powder-dry dust clouded around their heels; their leather sandals slapping the brittle, unyielding earth. But Elijah climbed with a promise from God in his heart: 'Go and present yourself to King Ahab... I will soon send rain!' (18:1). He had the promise, but he still had to possess the promise, for God was working in partnership with this man. I wonder how many times we frustrate God because we read and believe in the promises of Scripture, but we refuse to fulfil our part (for many of the promises of God come with clear conditions), or we don't wrestle in prayer in order to possess those blessings.

The lessons that Elijah had learned in the lonely years paid off now, because even though earlier in the day fire had jumped out of the sky the first time he asked for it, now he had to send his servant out seven times before receiving the weather report he wanted to hear.

Elijah didn't give up, but, to use an old term, 'he prayed through'.

And in his perseverance, he was gifted with an ability to sense, feel and hear what others could never perceive: 'I hear a mighty rainstorm coming!' But there was no audible sound to be heard.

There were no clouds in the sky and the distant sea remained a dazzling mirror, reflecting the deep blue of a cloudless sky. But Elijah heard something from God, and so the negative weather forecast didn't worry him at all.

At last, the servant reported a cloud-sighting. It seemed no bigger than a man's hand, but it was enough for Elijah.

He jumped up – a man utterly alive and bouncing with an exuberant, extravagant joy – and told his servant to rush down and tell the king to get himself home quickly, for the floods were coming.

Once again, the prophet was telling the
king what to do and when.

It was a sound piece of advice, for the ground had been
hard-baked for over three years. Water that would normally
seep down into thirsty sub-soil would not be able to break
through the concrete-like crust. Flash floods were inevitable.

-     -   -   -   -

It was a troubled, confused Ahab who ordered his
charioteers to head for home with speed.

As the fine Arabians were urged on faster by the whips
and screams of the horsemen, the king pondered the
sobering fact that his life had been turned upside down.

Why was it that Elijah seemed to be calling the shots at every
opportunity, telling him where to meet, and now when to eat?

He, Ahab, was king - wasn't he?

And then, a hideous, seeping fear that threatened to
totally overwhelm his mind began to take shape.

He had been visibly shaken when the fire came.

Could it *really* be that Yahweh was truly God after all?
If that was the case, then where did that leave him, a king
who had mocked Yahweh and led a nation after Baal?

Perhaps he thought about the executions of the Baal prophets.

He was no stranger to blood. He'd laughed when Jezebel
had sported by torturing some of Yahweh's servants,
and hadn't even flinched when finally they had been
beheaded in the palace courtyard - gory entertainment

for the day's end. It wasn't the wholesale slaughter of the Baal prophets that disturbed him – it was more the reaction that he anticipated would explode at home when his bride discovered what had happened.

Again, he must have wondered who exactly was in charge.

His wife?

The Tishbite?

Yahweh?

And then he heard the cry of his horseman, and followed his pointed finger.

Incredibly, it was Elijah, his camel skin cloak tucked up into his belt, running at such a speed that Ahab blinked twice in order to assure himself that, on this strangest of days, he was not hallucinating. It was no mirage. In fact, the glaring sun that had turned the land into a blast furnace for those last three years seemed to have died suddenly. It was as if a black storm was chasing Elijah as he came striding up towards the rattling, bumping royal chariot. And then, impossibly, the grinning prophet overtook the king – his strong, bronzed legs working like pistons, his breath punctuating the air in great, measured gasps.

His laughing eyes seemed ablaze with a power that sent a shudder down Ahab's spine. Off into the distance he sped, the king following.

There have been some commentators who have suggested that Elijah was out of the will of God by going back to Jezreel, and that his leaping like a gazelle past the king was a tacky display of pride. It was a work of the flesh, they suggest, that motivated Elijah to dash back to civilisation in order to bask in the spotlight of success and affirmation. To argue their case, they point to the fact that no direct instruction from God specifically ordering Elijah back to Jezreel is recorded in Scripture. He was acting in pride that contributed to the fall that was shortly to come.

I totally disagree with these negative analyses. Elijah had just come from the place of fervent prayer, and this was the kind of praying that brings three-year droughts to an instant, waterlogged conclusion. Elijah's running ability was supernaturally fuelled, probably unrivalled even in Olympic circles today.

Why was he able to cruise past the king's finest Arabians with ease? Scripture provides the answer: 'The hand of the Lord was upon him.' This is a term that denotes favour and blessing.

Surely Elijah went back to Jezreel under divine steam – and how very logical it was that he did so. The man had just presided over a gathering that had climaxed in a national cry of repentance, or so it seemed. Now he would need to be on hand, close to the corridors of power, in order to respond strategically to the unfolding events to come.

As the figure of Elijah became a dot in the distance and finally disappeared over a hill, it was as if the clouds exploded and great trapdoors suddenly sprang open, releasing millions of litres in a few moments, causing the ground itself to sizzle in shock. The drought was really over. Now what?

[1] A.W. Pink, *The Life of Elijah* (Edinburgh: Banner of Truth Trust), 1976, p246

Six:
PROPHET AT A LOSS

'When Ahab got home, he told Jezebel everything Elijah had done, including the way he had killed all the prophets of Baal. So Jezebel sent this message to Elijah: "May the gods strike me and even kill me if by this time tomorrow I have not killed you just as you killed them."

Elijah was afraid and fled for his life. He went to Beersheba, a town in Judah, and he left his servant there. Then he went on alone into the wilderness, traveling all day. He sat down under a solitary broom tree and prayed that he might die. "I have had enough, LORD," he said. "Take my life, for I am no better than my ancestors who have already died."

Then he lay down and slept under the broom tree. But as he was sleeping, an angel touched him and told him, "Get up and eat!" He looked around and there beside his head was some bread baked on hot stones and a jar of water! So he ate and drank and lay down again.

Then the angel of the LORD came again and touched him and said, "Get up and eat some more, or the journey ahead will be too much for you."' – 1 Kings 19:1-7

Those who believe they believe in God, but without passion in the heart, without anguish of mind, without uncertainty, without doubt, and even at times without despair, believe only in the idea of God, and not in God Himself.
(Madeleine L'Engle)[1]

Elijah returned to a virtually deserted Jezreel.

No crowds turned out to meet the new hero, because most were still struggling back through the waterlogged roads from Carmel – a journey that would take at least a couple of days.

Even the king was still en route. Jezreel was a veritable ghost town. Only the old people, too infirm to travel for the Carmel contest, plus those safe enough to ignore the royal decree, remained in the city.

And then there were probably those who were so committed to Baal that they remained behind, hoping that the fact that the Queen's decision not to appear, along with her entourage and the prophets of Asherah, would provide them with a political insurance policy.

Elijah found a place of lodging, and then waited.

It would not be long. Within twenty-four hours the first of the common people, exhausted from their journey, splattered and caked with mud, would have trailed their last few weary steps through the city gates, a glad smile on their faces.

It was good to be home. The king himself was back in the city too.

As Jezreel once again became a throbbing, thriving metropolis, Elijah became something of a celebrity. It became difficult for him to go out of his lodgings, with people wanting to talk to him everywhere he went – conversations that would have taken all day and all night. As he walked through the city, fingers pointed at him; children rushed up and grabbed his camel skin, eager to be around the famous man. How totally alive, he felt as if electricity was flowing through every nerve in his body.

His mind was racing, packed full of ideas.

At long last, the people had rejected the Baals, and now further action would need to be taken. It was reformation time.

He pondered the events to come, imagining with relish the wonder of Israel walking hand in hand with the true God once again.

There would be a summons to the palace.

Surely the chastened king would be eager to consult with the prophet of Yahweh, now that God Himself had so powerfully vindicated His servant.

A season of repentance and fasting would be ordered by royal decree.

Units of the army would be sent up and down the nation to seek out and destroy the Baal altars and bring any resident Baal prophets to justice.

The Asherah prophets would have to be dealt with.

Legislation would be handed down from the king to prevent the curse of Baalism ever rising again in Israel. Perhaps there would be a public reading of the Law, and a rededication of all of the male children who had been dedicated by circumcision to Baal.

It was all too wonderful, a dream come true. Repeatedly Elijah allowed his imagination to go wild as he considered the bright and glorious days ahead. God was continuing to kiss the ground with rain; the smile of Yahweh spread broadly over Israel again.

Yet one nagging, lurking thought remained.

Jezebel.

Born and raised in the service of Baal. Murderess of the prophets, exterminator of the schools.

Would she turn too?

—   —   —   —   —

Deep in the heart of the palace, in the Queen's bed chamber, paced a furious Jezebel.

Her usually beautiful face was a twisted, snarling mask of ugly rage; her fists clenched until her knuckles stood out white as she marched up and down the fabulous room. She had tried to control herself when her snivelling, pathetic little husband had told her all that Elijah had done.

He must have thought her to be so very stupid.

Of course, she noticed that he had carefully avoided all mention of Yahweh, knowing that to use that name was not good for peace.
Instead he had centred his words on the actions of the prophet from Gilead. When she heard about his mocking of the Baal priests, she became enraged. She struggled to maintain her composure, locking her facial muscles into a look of quiet interest as her husband spoke. But when she heard about the Kishon massacre, she felt her head swimming with a blind, insane hatred. Unable to contain

herself any longer, she made her excuses and rushed out
of the throne room to the safety of her private chambers.

Now, one solitary thought dominated all others: the desire for
vengeance. She would get even, and in doing so, she would wipe
the memory of this fire-breathing prophet from Israel for ever.
He would die after hours of begging for death, to end the terrible
torture she had in mind for him. With a scream that demanded
instant attention, or else, she summoned her servants.

–   –   –   –   –

Perhaps he was sleeping when it happened –
dreaming of drought, fire and death.

Perhaps in his vivid nightmare the lifeless eyes of 450 stared
accusingly at him, their bodies suddenly coming to life
again – the broken, bloodied Baal priests stirring, a satanic
resurrection, rising again to march back in triumph to Jezreel...

Suddenly, the royal messenger was framed in the doorway;
his chest heaving from the run, a hint of mockery in
his eyes. Elijah wearily shook his head as if to shake off
fatigue in a moment, and wiped the sleep from his eyes.

Elijah carefully searched his face for a hint of the words to come. Obviously enjoying his brief moment of power, the messenger took his time.

Patiently the prophet waited.

'You've gone too far this time, Tishbite. I've seen Her
Majesty in a temper before, but never like this. Never.'

The envoy paused and remembered, and then the arrogance was gone and his eyes clouded with fear as he recalled the scene back at the palace. 'When the king told her about Carmel, and about how you killed her prophets, she flew into such a rage, I swear that her personal attendants were all beside themselves with terror. And then she went quiet for a long time. I'm not sure which was worse: the screaming or the silence.'

Tiredness seemed suddenly to overwhelm Elijah's body, and with it came a growing, gnawing sense of fear about what was to come. He didn't have to wait long. The royal envoy continued, his words deliberate, slow, in order to maximise their effect.

'The Queen called her friends together and said that she had a very important vow to swear, and that everybody was to witness it. She screamed out the names of her gods at the top of her voice, ran her finger across her throat, and carefully pronounced the self-curse. She told me to repeat it to you very carefully, Elijah. Word for word.'

The servant straightened himself up as if to deliver a formal sentence.

'May the gods strike me and even kill me, if by this time tomorrow I have not killed you just as you killed them.'

Suddenly the messenger was gone, the echo of his words ringing in the chamber. What was it she had said? 'If I I have not killed you just as you killed them.'

The imagery was chilling, as he remembered the killing field called Kishon. Bloodied bodies piled high, corpse upon corpse, eyes staring – a hill of death. 'Like one of them...'

Suddenly, uncontrollably, he began to shake.

–　　　–　　　–　　　–　　　–

Why did the queen send a messenger to Elijah with an announcement of his forthcoming death?

She could have just despatched an assassin to get the job done immediately. She had put all the other prophets to death, so why not just go ahead and kill Elijah? To warn him was to take the risk that he would run (as indeed he did). So why the death threat instead of death itself?

It's possible that she sent a message rather than a hired hit-man because she knew that, despite her great power, she would be going too far if she actually killed Elijah.

I doubt that she feared her husband. Perhaps, for the first time, she feared the common people. If they could turn on the prophets of Baal, they could storm the palace as well if she murdered their hero.

Or was there a more subtle reason behind her strategy?

Perhaps Jezebel opted for the messenger because she had discovered a satanic secret weapon. Certainly it would take a special attack to bring this hitherto invincible man down. He had stood before the highest authority in the land and denounced him. He had challenged four hundred witches, knowing the dark power that was theirs, a gift from devils rather than gods. It was time to use the weapon that she had triumphed with repeatedly down through her dark years.

Fear.

A threat or a suggestion of terrors to come is often more intimidating than the action itself. She would manipulate the man from Gilead with words – clutch hold of his soul and hang on with a vice-like grip, and cause him to destroy himself. And what a master she was in the evil art of manipulation.

The Septuagint version includes Jezebel adding to the message: 'As sure as I am Jezebel, and you are Elijah.'

These were carefully chosen words, proclaiming her royalty, power and importance ('I am Jezebel') and her enemy's nothingness, in human terms – a mere peasant from the hills ('you are Elijah'). She was ripping his sense of God-given identity right out of his soul. It was a brilliant tactic – inspiration from hell itself. And it worked.

-        -   -   -   -

In a few seconds, an awful metamorphosis surged through Elijah's heart and mind with such a force that he seemed to become a different man altogether. The ballistic missile called fear vaporised in a second the memory of all that God had done for and through Elijah. He became like a staggering insomniac, shocked into forgetting everything he had so painstakingly learned.

It was all wiped away, seemingly erased.

His prophecy about the drought, and the blistering years that followed.

Raven waiters.

Flour and oil that did not run out, and then resurrection for a sick boy in Zarephath.

Fire-bolts from the shimmering blue sky at Carmel.

Drought-shattering downpours, just because he had summoned them.

Bionic marathon running that put the
royal charioteers to shame.

All these episodes were part of his history,
they were all very real, but the reality was
shattered by a venomous dart called fear.

Then the man who had stood strong in his God on
Carmel tumbled down into a spiritual and psychological
pit – bottomless and dark. A place where hope,
laughter, vision and God Himself are all dead.

He should have stood his ground. Like a long-
distance runner who completes twenty-six miles and
then stops just short of the finishing tape, he was a
winner almost to the end – and then he snapped.

He should have taken the attitude of the ancient
character Chrysostom, who was also sent a
threatening letter by the Empress Eudoxia, and his
reply was, 'Go tell her I fear nothing but sin.'

But he didn't do the right thing, the heroic thing.

Fuelled by a mad, illogical panic, he ran. And how he ran!

Elijah staggered in a blind fog for a day's journey, desperate
for safety, only to then turn around and pray for death. But
this was no short-lived thing; a brief overnight stay in the
smothering hold of depression. It was far more serious than
that. He sent his faithful servant away, and then embarked
on a lengthy solitary trek through the wilderness.

The journey should not have taken him anywhere
near that long, unless he got hopelessly lost.

What went through his tortured
mind during those long, searing

furnace days, and those crushing, lonely nights when he lay under the stars, hearing only the plaintive wailing of jackals?

Did he wonder about the Hebrews who had tramped these sands for 40 years so long ago?

Where was the pillar of cloud that had greeted their waking?

Where was the blazing pillar of fire that had lit up their dark nights? Deep, hopeless despair etched into his face as he wearily continued; a man in mourning, grieving the death of his soul, and of his God.

Freeze the frame for a moment.

Stop with me and see an amazing, pitiful sight: the hero of Carmel now a suicidal fugitive; the prophet who rebuked a diabolical dictator king now scurrying away like a frightened rat scared by a flashlight. The question has to be asked: Why? What were the fatal flaws that caused this cataclysmic collapse? Perhaps the first crack didn't appear just because of fear, or even disappointment with the perilous circumstances that he found himself in, but rather because of a deeper disappointment - one that comes to most people of faith at some time or another.

Perhaps the man of God was disappointed with God.

-    -   -   -   -

When great hopes and dreams are shattered in a moment, depression quickly settles in on the human soul.

The bride who spends months anticipating and preparing for her wedding, only to stand in the entrance of a crowded church and be told that the man whom she thought was hers is not planning to attend the ceremony – ever – knows the excruciating emptiness of joy murdered by despair.

The woman who delivers her child after nine long wearisome months; whose eyes brighten with the thrill and anticipation of seeing her son or daughter for the first time, only to be told that her love is still-born – she knows the ecstasy and then the agony.

Elijah knew that kind of pain. He had breathed the air of hope deep into his soul – had felt that a new day had dawned after hundreds of years of blackest night – only to be told that the revival was hereby cancelled by royal decree.

There would be no turning, no revolution: the disgusting status quo was to continue.

Nothing could ever reach the heart of Jezebel – that dung-woman. He'd followed God's instructions to the letter – and it was all one great terrible, exhausting failure.

Ever felt like that?

The chances are that if you have, you kept the thoughts and feelings that nagged away at you very carefully hidden. The truth is that there are times when God seems to let us down.

We pray.
And pray.

We try to stir our hearts to faith, and hope for a miracle begins to form. We begin to be confident that God is going to work just as we have asked Him to – that He will respond to operate according to our plan. Plan A we'll call it.

There are times, however, when Plan A doesn't ever materialise. To put it bluntly, God has a habit of being God, and acting like God, and that means there are times when He has another plan – Plan B, if you like.

Elijah was a Plan A man. He had read and rehearsed and prayed and fasted through that plan until he knew it backwards: Ahab and Jezebel would lead the nation in repentance, and so on.

God, however, had another plan, and Ahab and Jezebel had no part in it. He was writing them out of the script altogether.

Jezebel, particularly, was beyond redemption. She had a callous heart that had been unmoved as the little children begged for mercy before the sacrificial fires. No firebolt from heaven was ever going to get her attention, and God knew that. He had other plans that were far more radical and revolutionary than Elijah could have imagined, and the wretched, pathetic royal family had been given their last chance already. Now they were written out of the screenplay for good as far as God was concerned.

As we will see later, the Lord had another person waiting in the wings – someone prepared and anointed and ready to reign.

However, like you and me, Elijah hadn't read that script. (I'm glad that God keeps a lot of the future hidden from us too. There may well be some things out on the horizon that I'd rather be totally ignorant of right now.)

God could have told Elijah some of His alternative plan – enough to help him to stand firm during this emotional hurricane, if he had just waited long enough to listen. But fear is deafening. It screams in our ears and drowns out even God's voice.

Perhaps a day or two of quiet reflection would have enabled Elijah to tune out the distortion and interference that screamed in his ears, and enabled him to realise that Jezebel's threat was little more than idle chatter. (Later, when Elijah appeared in public again and she had the opportunity to fulfil her threat, she never did so.)

But he didn't stop long enough to hear the real voice of authority, and so confusion and fear took control.

There are times in life when two plus two seems to equal five, when all the wonderful truths that we believe seem to turn to dust, or writing on yellowing canvas that stands only to mock us rather than comfort us.

And the temptation is to run from God – to flee. No amount of clever little sayings or clichés will keep us anchored. But it's trust – that quiet but desperate handhold – which causes us to cry out with Job, 'Though he slay me, yet will I hope in him' (Job 13:15, NIV). Trust will keep our feet anchored. But Elijah forgot that, and waved goodbye to God – and friendship too.

–   –   –   –   –

The long months spent at Zarephath had been designed to teach Elijah the value of warm human relationships. The isolation and exile of Kerith were only a temporary phase. But now, as he reached the limits of his strength, just when he needed the comfort and encouragement that true friendship brings, Elijah dismissed his servant, as I mentioned earlier. Some commentators have applauded this as a noble act, believing that the prophet sent his unnamed friend back to civilisation because he wanted to spare him a tiresome hike through the inhospitable desert with a prophet (retired) who would have been quite hopeless at conversation.

But as Elijah left his servant at Beersheba, which was very likely a city of refuge, I believe that he rejected a vital resource when he launched out stubbornly on his own. And the word that God spoke to him later, encouraging him that there were actually seven thousand faithful left in Israel, and instructing him to anoint Elisha as prophet to join him, seems to confirm my suspicion.

Elijah desperately needed friends.

He tried to carry a huge load upon his shoulders single-handedly – and like a champion weightlifter who manages for a while to hold up an impossible burden, his arms shaking with strain, blood vessels and veins popping out on his blood-filled face, he suddenly snapped. The champion of Carmel collapsed.

Nothing has changed.

I am constantly meeting Christians who are dying of terminal loneliness – and some of the worst cases of this ancient and modern disease are to be found among leaders.

Too many times I have sat in homes and restaurants with Christian leaders, some successful (whatever that means), others struggling. All who smile brightly in public, talk eloquently about love and the blessings of fellowship, but have broken down and wept like babies when asked who their friends are.

In some cases the fault lies with education and training. Years ago, many students studying theology in preparation for the traditional clergy model of ministry were taught that it is inappropriate to have friendship with people who are part of the congregation they lead, lest others consider that they are favouring one member of the church over another.

Things have changed, thankfully, but perhaps the false notion still lingers in some circles. The Church is a family, not a corporation. Why should leaders be motivated and dominated by the immature jealousy of others? Envy needs to be repented of, not pandered to.

Jesus modelled relational leadership among a group of disciples who were highly prone to pettiness and jealousy. It was His hand-picked twelve who argued about who would get the best seats in the kingdom of heaven. It was the twelve who wanted to call down fire from heaven on anybody who did signs and wonders but were not part of their outfit.

They wanted to franchise the kingdom.

But in an atmosphere where He could have so easily been misunderstood and criticised, Jesus had His own small group of particularly close friendships.

That group was a triumvirate: Peter, James and John.

They had front row seats for the transfiguration. Only they were allowed in when Jesus raised Peter's mother-in-law – the others were left to stand outside (probably complaining about the injustice of their being excluded).

And it was the famous three who were invited to go forward with Jesus in Gethsemane and watch with Him as He knelt in agonised prayer. Of the three, John seems singled out as the one closest to Him – 'the disciple whom Jesus loved'.

Are there Christian leaders around the world right now who are expected to preach like Spurgeon, have the wisdom of Solomon, nurture perfect families, pray powerfully, and yet have no one to share their fears, doubts and sins with?

-     -   -   -   -

Elijah dismissed his servant, and did what so many of us modern believers do when we go through trials and difficulty. Instead of crying out for help and standing our ground, we run for our lives, only to find that even when we get somewhere else, nothing has changed, for we have taken ourselves, our attitudes, our problems and our sins along with us for the ride.

So Elijah runs for his life – and then prays for death. The scenery was very different. He was in an area that was beyond the rule of Ahab, so technically he was safe. But within him still beat a heart paralysed by fear – and he couldn't run from that.

Elijah ran into a wilderness of despair because he saw death in Jezebel's message – and he saw the end of his own calling and ministry as well.

It was all over simply because he received a note. And the man who had forgotten so much about God in a few fear-filled seconds finally broke down and forgot who he himself was. No longer was he the chosen of Yahweh, the fearless anointed. He was robbed of identity by his own terror, and he complained that he was no better than his ancestors (who, by the way, aren't even named in the Bible). He threw everything away in response to one action instigated with brilliant cunning by Jezebel.

I can identify with Elijah.

There have been too many times when I have felt like giving up my calling to ministry because of one single, isolated incident that made me say, 'That's it! It's all over.' Or, with Elijah, I've yelled at God and anyone else who might happen to be listening, 'I have had enough!'

How grateful I am that God gave me a wife in Kay: someone who can help me gain perspective when I am tempted to overreact.

When I was a pastor, I remember storming into our house one dark Monday morning. After a difficult weekend, someone had made what I felt to be an unkind remark at the office, and it was to me the proverbial straw that broke the camel's back. Kay was reading something as I rushed in, and I yelled at the top of my voice, 'That's *it*! I am resigning!'

She carried on reading.

I was irritated beyond belief.

Here I was, limping pathetically in the shadow of death, or so I thought, and she had nothing to say.

I repeated the statement again, with increased decibels. Silence.

For the third time I repeated my statement of defeat, by now desperate for a reaction. I got one. Without looking up, Kay said, 'You don't even know how to spell resignation.'

It was just what I needed.

- - - - -

Elijah had been called to do all kinds of very difficult things in his life, but never once do we hear him complain – until now.

And how he complains. It's as if a great plaintive wail rises from his heart, as a paralysing self-pity that locks his mind and freezes his heart possesses him.

Over breakfast, God asks him, 'What are you doing here?'

His response: 'I have been very zealous for the LORD God Almighty. The Israelites have rejected your covenant, broken down your altars, and put your prophets to death with the sword. I am the only one left, and now they are trying to kill me too' (1 Kings 19:10, NIV).

Twice Elijah repeats his little speech word for word in the hearing of God. His mind is locked solidly on a single track which he seems unable to break out of. At least he is being honest about his feelings, but he is only partly right: self-pity has a way of distorting our perception.

Listen more closely to his speech:

'I have been very zealous.' (True enough, Elijah. You really have done well up to now. But just one little point: why are you saying it in your whiny, complaining tone of voice? Doesn't God know that you've been zealous? Do you regret the level of commitment that you've offered to him?)

'The Israelites have rejected your covenant, broken down your altars.' (Yes, they have, but what about Carmel? The altar was rebuilt there. Yes, Jezebel is as stubborn as ever, but does that mean that the whole nation is going to follow in her wicked footsteps?)

'...and put your prophets to death with the sword.' (Actually, it was that one woman who commanded that... remember? Perhaps those in the atrocity obeyed because of terror. But the whole nation had not turned against the prophets.)

'I am the only one left.' (That's just flat wrong. There are actually still seven thousand faithful in Israel. You're not on your own at all, Elijah. You just feel that way because you dismissed your servant and are now in the twilight zone of self-imposed solitary confinement.)

'...and now they are trying to kill me too.' (Jezebel is, Elijah – not 'they'.)

Self-pity blurs our ability to see clearly.

Never make a significant decision about life when you are meandering around in the fog of self-pity. Such decision-making will inevitably lead to disaster.

- - - - -

Elijah forgets God, self – and common sense. So dark is his despair that he neglects even the basic necessities of life, like food and drink.

His only prayer is for a sleep from which he will never wake up. So an angel is hastily despatched to cook for the worn out (and by now malnourished) man of God. Notice that the angel touches him (twice in fact), but this is not a miraculous touch that spiritually turbo-charges him. Rather, it's a wake-up call from God – a nudge from the heavenlies to announce that breakfast is cooked and waiting to be eaten. This was an act of great tenderness.

No angels appeared to Elijah during his heady days on Carmel; no supernatural being cooked a celebratory supper when the sickly child was raised back in Zarephath. But now the man who thinks that the dried bones of his grandparents are worth more than he is gets to meet one of God's supernatural warriors.

Yet this was more than tender care: this was a deeply practical act. Elijah certainly needed the power of the Holy Spirit to flood his life afresh, but he also needed a couple of good, wholesome meals in his stomach, for 'the journey is too much for [him]'. Some of his depression was rooted in the fact that he had been overtaxing himself and obviously not taking care of his body.

–   –   –   –   –

Days of raging sunshine snapping and licking
at his neck, searching for flesh.

Three hundred weary miles through
the searing Sinai Peninsula.

Like a blind man lost, he struggled, desperately trying
to suppress the death wish. This was a stubborn
despair. Even a visit from an angel disguised as a fast-
food chef didn't shift the jet-black cloud in his heart.

Onwards he stumbled through the sand all day, stopping in the afternoon heat to rest. At night he slept with tears damp on his face; his mind frantically fighting off vivid visions of armies of demons – all of them pointing at him, the ex-champion. Every night the dream was the same. They just stood there, lines of them: black, impish accusers. And they said nothing.

They just pointed gnarled fingers at him... and laughed.

[1] Madeleine L'Engle, *Walking on Water: Reflections on Faith and Art* (Colorado Springs, CO: WaterBrook Press, 2001) p28

Seven:
FAITHFUL GOD

'So he got up and ate and drank, and the food gave him enough strength to travel forty days and forty nights to Mount Sinai, the mountain of God. There he came to a cave, where he spent the night.

But the LORD said to him, "What are you doing here, Elijah?"

Elijah replied, "I have zealously served the LORD God Almighty. But the people of Israel have broken their covenant with you, torn down your altars, and killed every one of your prophets. I am the only one left, and now they are trying to kill me, too."

"Go out and stand before me on the mountain," the LORD told him. And as Elijah stood there, the LORD passed by, and a mighty windstorm hit the mountain. It was such a terrible blast that the rocks were torn loose, but the LORD was not in the wind. After the wind there was an earthquake, but the LORD was not in the earthquake. And after the earthquake there was a fire, but the LORD was not in the fire. And after the fire there was the sound of a gentle whisper. When Elijah heard it, he wrapped his face in his cloak and went out and stood at the entrance of the cave.

And a voice said, "What are you doing here, Elijah?"

He replied again, "I have zealously served the LORD God Almighty. But the people of Israel have broken their covenant with you, torn down your altars, and killed every one of your prophets. I am the only one left, and now they are trying to kill me, too."

Then the LORD told him, "Go back the same way you came, and travel to the wilderness of Damascus. When you arrive there, anoint Hazael to be king of Aram. Then anoint Jehu grandson of Nimshi to be king of Israel, and anoint Elisha son of Shaphat from the town of Abel-meholah to replace you as my prophet. Anyone who escapes from Hazael will be killed by Jehu, and those who escape Jehu will be killed by Elisha! Yet I will preserve 7,000 others in Israel who have never bowed down to Baal or kissed him!"' – 1 Kings 19:8-18

Beersheba had been a haven in more ways than one.

The land there was lush and fertile – a broad, inviting valley. As Elijah headed due south, and the landscape became barren, bleak and treeless, it seemed that the changing scenery more accurately reflected the state of his heart.

Scattered rocks strewn around only momentarily irritated him by day. However, as dusk slowly extinguished the flaming westbound sun, it brought relief from the furnace heat, but the rocks became his enemies, tripping and cutting his feet in the moonless black.

Perhaps it had always been in his heart to head towards Mount Sinai.

Perhaps during those long, lonely days an impression began to form in his heart; a magnet drawing him, pulling him, causing him to wonder if this was indeed *the voice* again.

It couldn't be.

He had failed miserably – he was a disgrace to God and Israel. And yet the tugging grew stronger until he knew that not only should he go to Sinai, but he should go to the cave that Moses reputedly stood in when the Lord passed by so many years earlier. (The Hebrew text reveals that Elijah went to 'the' cave – presumably a reference to the Cave of Moses.)

Could it possibly be that the God who had shown Himself to the mighty Moses might actually do something similar for a suicidal depressive called Elijah?

It was but a tiny spark, a faint flicker of hope that glimmered in his heart. But, like a man cupping a campfire flame, protecting it from the threatening wind, he nursed that hope carefully and began the journey to the Mountain of Moses.

He took the westward road to Kadesh-Barnea, a town on the perimeter of the Sinai Desert, a last outpost of life before the dreadful dustbowl began. It was a place where men would thoroughly pick the minds of the local Bedouins, frantically trying to gather information about trails and landmarks in the great Sinai desert.

The very fact that Elijah would step out into the wilderness alone shows us the urgent desperation of the man. He just had to know the embrace of God again, so he was willing to launch out into a hauntingly deceptive place – a land of old ghosts, where a whole nation got lost for two decades. Even the most desolate place is warmed by the presence of friends, fellow travellers. The Israelites of old wandered in the Sinai desert with God as their guide and with the comforting soundtrack of the voices and laughter of a crowd of millions.

As Elijah looked out across the powder-sky furnace that was Sinai, there must have been natural apprehension in his heart.

Would the leather-lined faces of the Kadesh Bedouins be the last human beings he would ever see? Would he become just another skeleton, an ugly skull-smile picked at by scavenger birds and jackals, a monument to sober other travellers? Whatever the risk, he knew somehow that he had to do it, for life without God was living death, and Mount Sinai was his last, desperate hope.

So Elijah went out there alone. Six long weeks of empty wandering: searing heat in the morning, longing for the reliable relief of the afternoon breezes, disappointment as the sun dived for cover each day leaving the sharp chill of the night.

Think of it. Put yourself in his sandals: 40 long days of trudging despair.

This was no Kerith, for at Kerith there had been God, and though there was so much silence, it was a pregnant quiet, a purposeful isolation.

Down through the trackless Plain of Tih he went.

Those were the longest days of his life. Then he saw the chaotic mass of peaks that was Sinai, away in the distance – granite savagely slashing the brilliant blue sky. Perhaps then he knew the disappointment that seeps into us when we discover that most things are not quite as good as they were anticipated to be. Sinai was undeniably striking, quite beautiful, but just... ordinary.

No cloud of glory.

No booming voice of God.

No dancing dramatic lightning bolts.

Perhaps he stood at the north end of the Plain of Rahah, where Israel had gathered to hear Moses read the Law to Israel. Did he imagine the millions of his ancestors standing there, covenant-makers of history? Did he perhaps yell out the commandments, fascinated by the sound of his own voice echoing around the plateau, disappointed that the only voice he could hear was his own?

What had happened to that other voice? Where had God gone?

Finally, after meandering around the mountain for days, he decided to climb higher and go to the cave where Moses was alleged to have resided when he spent 40 days in communion with God.

Like a pilgrim at an ancient shrine, Elijah went in and laid down. It was all a waste – the journey had been futile.

He was at the most sacred spot he could imagine, and it was all too obvious. The God of Moses was gone.

Or so he thought.

Look at him.

There he sits, hunched in the corner of a dingy cave roughly gouged out of the mountainside. The man who had stood in the finest home in Israel and rebuked the owner is holed up, seated on a carpet of dried bat's droppings; arms hugging his knees, which are drawn up to his chest in the foetal position. His face is buried, pressed down hard on knees and forearms; his knotted, bedraggled black hair a chaotic mop. No sound. Only the shuddering, shaking shoulders tell you that he is crying again. A man at the end of himself, starved of hope.

Can we identify with him, as he longs to rekindle
life and faith, but doesn't know how?

Have you wandered back to places – church buildings, cities,
homes – where many years ago you possessed a simple
trust in God that was so uncluttered and uncomplicated?

Where is your Sinai?

For me, in the early years of my Christian life, it was a
small, functional park in Ilford, where I would spend every
lunch break from the office. I would go there each day and
sit on the same bench with the warmth of the sun on my
back, or in a shelter in the winter. There I eagerly devoured
chapter after chapter of the Bible, revelling in the thrill of
new discovery. Prayer was easy, and any struggle I put
down to the fact that I was a 'new babe' in the faith.

There were many questions, but it seemed so easy
just to deal with anything that I didn't understand
by a quick shrug of the shoulders and a child-like
prayer: 'Oh well, Lord, I'll just trust you anyway...'

It was first love – virginal, untouched by the erosion of cynicism.
I didn't know back then that some preachers waxed eloquent
on Sundays and lived very different lives on Mondays. I didn't
know about the churches that displayed 'God is love' posters
on their buildings and then fought and gossiped and split, and
did so in the name of God. No, back then, every Christian was
still a wonderful, pure person; another member of my new
family. My love was untainted by hypocrisy or disappointment.
I had no experience of 'sheep shock' – the discovery that
Christians fail and sin like everybody else. That park was
my Sinai; the place where I first got acquainted with God.

Perhaps your condition is far more serious, and you can relate
to the Sinaitic caveman more closely. For you, God has become

little more than a theory, a doctrinal idea, a cause, a reason for the morality programme that you call your Christianity. You attend church, and perhaps it's good, lively and creative, but it feels like going to a birthday party every week, only you forgot whose birthday it is. The truths that you have committed yourself to begin to sound like hollow slogans. You knot your brow with intense concentration during the worship time, and do your best to imagine dark Calvary hillsides during communion, but perhaps you feel like this prophet. It's not that you can even blame your church, for it is widely regarded as a good church. But the question nags, the unspeakable gnawing:

Where is God?

Where is the God of Elijah?

Be honest. What would you expect God to do with a man like this?

Pension him off?

Judge him for failure and cowardice?

Worse even than that, maybe just leave him alone, ignore him, let him die in the dampness of the cave? The Lord chose none of these available options. I'm still discovering that God is better and kinder than I ever imagined him to be. Perhaps that's one reason why eternity really does mean for ever and ever – so that God can show His 'immeasurable kindness to us in Christ Jesus'. The Lord knew just what Elijah needed.

–   –   –   –   –

Truth sets us free, particularly from fear. As we've already noted, Elijah was labouring with an exaggerated perception of his problem.

Fear has the ability to amplify and enlarge the size of real problems way beyond their actual size. In some cases I have met Christians who have spent years in what can only be described as futile shadow-boxing – dodging and weaving and defending themselves against nothing more than the power of their own vivid imaginations.

Of course, shadow-boxing can be just as demanding and exhausting as the real thing.

Fear became an obsessive part of Elijah's thought patterns. His mind was locked in fear – always walking down the same mental pathway, round and round in anxiety-filled circles. To refer for a moment to ancient technology, have you ever heard a record player stylus get stuck in the groove? Remember the infuriating repetitiveness, as one phrase or three notes are repeated over and over and over again, until mercifully someone taps the needle gently and moves it along to the next phrase of the song?

This was Elijah's mind.

And so God asked the question: 'What are you doing here?'

The question was to be asked again later. Look at Scripture, and you'll find that Elijah gave the Lord exactly the same answer, word for word, twice over. Mentally, the stylus was stuck, and Elijah was on a railway track of predictable, well-worn thought processes that would ultimately drive him over the brink to the abyss of utter despair – unless someone jogged the needle.

That is why God asked the question. Did God need an answer for his own benefit? No. Man looks at the outside, but God looks at the heart. God knew.

The question was an invitation. 'Elijah. Talk to me! Throw aside your nice pleasant speech and just tell me what's going on in that locked mind of yours.'

God knew, but he wanted Elijah to get all those pent-up feelings and emotions out into the open.

Elijah's response shows us that he was not afraid to speak his mind to God.

Remember, this man had seen nuclear-fission-type fire snap suddenly out of the heavens; he had stood back and watched the sizzling of the water being instantly evaporated by the white-hot heat that shot laser-like from the finger of God. He knew that he was dealing with someone of *real* power – one who could crumple the planet in His hand in a second and toss it aside like a spoiled paper – but still vented his frustration.

Be honest with God. Tell Him what you really think. He knows your heart anyway. Sometimes I think that we pray our poetic, flowing stanzas, frustrating the God who longs for us to just say what's really on our minds and in our hearts.

Beware of compulsive self-talk too.

When I first became a Christian I was so desperate to do the will of God that I became obsessed with the fear of making a mistake. I bought books on the subject (and there were plenty available – it took me forever to decide which ones it was God's will for me to read). I prayed, I fasted, I tried to work out the significance of my circumstances. I cross-examined my heart to check if I had real confirmatory peace. Peace, I was told, was supposed to supernaturally accompany every decision, like an umpire who confirms a call in sport. The scriptural basis for this was Colossians 3:15, where it says: 'Let the peace of Christ rule in your hearts' (NIV). Every book I read suggested that this meant that this subjective feeling should be the final indicator that all is well in God's sight. Quite apart from the fact that Colossians 3 is an exhortation on relational difficulties in the local church, and has nothing whatever to do with personal guidance, I was so terrified I might not have enough peace that I was in a total state of panic anyway.

I asked other believers for advice – and my fear increased. I was unable to make decisions lest I made a mistake and be consigned to the terrifying scrap heap unhelpfully designated by fiery preachers as 'God's second best'. A thousand times I travelled a well-worn mental trail, repeating over and over my reasons for what I was doing – particularly in challenging meetings. Looking back, I feel that I came close to a breakdown. Someone had to jog the needle for me, and let me know that the will of God was not designed to be a baffling jigsaw puzzle with fiendish forfeits for those who make a mistake.

But it was compulsive, almost obsessive thinking that got me into such a state. Such was the thinking of Elijah – hence God's kindly cross-examination.

The question was also a revelation: 'What are you doing here, Elijah?' God uses his servant's name. In some ways, that's natural enough – to use someone's name is an expression of tenderness and care. But remember the meaning of that name: Eli-yah – 'the Lord, He is the real God'. Now rephrase that into the question. To a man in a self-imposed solitary confinement, miles from where he had been called to be, crumpled by despair, terrified by thoughts of suicide, God says, 'What are you doing here, the Lord, He is the real God?'

God knows the power of gentle, subtle irony, but judging by his servant's response, the pun was too subtle for Elijah.

God is speaking. Elijah sits still, fixed, unmovable, unresponsive. So a cosmic firework display begins. Scripture records that 'God was not in' the wind, earthquake and fire that follow – but He did allow this eruption of attention-grabbing natural phenomena to break out.

I'm amazed at the faith of Elijah on Carmel. I'm even more stunned at his hard-hearted attitude on Sinai.

First of all a hurricane-level wind of unprecedented strength whips up, and it is so mighty that it breaks rocks. Now Elijah's cave becomes a wind tunnel; his hair, a mane standing on end, his cloak, a flag whipping and reeling around his legs. Naturally speaking, it's hardly surprising that Elijah stays put, for the cave would have offered some protection from the terrifying blast. But God had said: 'Come out – I'm here.' Was this a reminder to Elijah that he had been called to obedience, even if it meant a lifetime spent facing the winds of popular opinion, the hurricanes of murderous threats of powerful men and women smashing into his face?

Elijah had been called to stand firm in the face of hurricane Jezebel and had failed. He stays put in his cave, battered by the storm and six paces from God's embrace. All he has to do is step out.

Stage two of the display begins now.

Just when the prophet begins to feel relief because the terrifying winds are beginning to subside, a stomach-churning earthquake begins. Now this really is a prod from God. Evacuate, Elijah.

Get out of there!

You shouldn't linger in caves during an earthquake – to state the obvious, they might cave in.

The ground trembles and churns and boils, and Elijah stays put.

His will withstands the voice of God, the mighty wind and the restless upheaval of the earth. He's not coming out.

Stage three, the final scenario: fire. This was familiar territory, prompting memories of the Carmel that was just weeks earlier, but had seemed like years ago – or had it really happened? Did Elijah go through that doubt-amnesia that causes us to question even the greatest examples of God's grace and intervention in our lives? Just as the bolt from the Canaan blue had been designed to confirm the reality of the true, living God to an entire nation, so this personal fire licks thirstily around the cave specifically to confirm the struggling faith of one lonely man.

Wind that turned the desert into a sand-blaster.

The earth in convulsions.

Furnace-hot flames out of thin air.

And one stationary Elijah, who still won't venture out.

Then a voice speaks inside that cave, and the voice succeeds where all the other natural displays failed. Was God showing

Elijah that the ability to hear the voice of God is greater than the ability to take authority over the forces of nature? God was about to speak and declare a strategy that would succeed where the fire of Carmel had failed. We will never know what God said in that moment – Scripture only records that He spoke, not the words that He said.

I've speculated at length as to why it is that no more detail is recorded, considering the fact that the word or words God spoke succeeded in convincing Elijah that he really ought to obey Yahweh and walk five steps to the mouth of the cave. Perhaps, despite the stark focus in which Elijah's downfall is portrayed, God determined to pull a veil of privacy over this most intimate moment of His friendship with Elijah.

Whatever the dialogue, it worked. Elijah made his choice: it was time to start talking to God again.

God is omnipresent. That means that He is everywhere all of the time, and that, presumably, includes caves. God was in there with Elijah – so why invite the prophet to step outside 'because [my] presence is about to pass by' (NIV)?

Why not light up the musty darkness with a divine sparkler, or write a message of love on the wall of the cave – the finger of God extended?

Surely the call to step outside had nothing to do with location.

It was an invitation to choose, to take a step, to engage the will.

Granted, God baited the invitation very heavily with an almost irresistible wooing: 'The presence of the Lord is passing by...'

The God of Kerith, Zarephath, Carmel, and yes Elijah, even Samaria with its whore-groves (where you could rent a prostitute who would tell you that you were doing the gods a service as well as yourself): that God of *everywhere* was passing by.

Fundamentally this was all about choices. Elijah, choose. On Carmel, you called a nation to choose. Now you do the same.

The God of wind, earthquakes and fire can do all manner of incredible things. He can cause a colourful universe to jump into existence, just because He says so.

He can instruct the sun to stand still in time and space for an hour or two.

He can listen and respond to the hearts of millions of His praying people, all at the same time.

He can hire and fire kings and princes as He chooses, and weave a plan to redeem humankind through what seemed like a fly-blown execution outside the city walls of Jerusalem.

When it comes to miracle-working and making the impossible spring into reality, God can do it all.

Yet there's one thing He cannot, *will not* do.

He won't make our minds up for us. He won't overrule the dignity and depravity of the human will. We always have a choice. God refuses to dehumanise the crown of His creation – humankind – by taking away our right to choose, and that commitment is eternal.

Only when Elijah stepped out did God give some further instruction and strategy: Elijah had to respond before the next steps could be revealed.

I have seen too many Christians almost destroy their lives because they refused to make the right choices. Such is the case with one man I know who has attended a lively evangelical church for many years – and still has a huge problem with pornography and prostitutes. Every time I see him I hear the same story: 'I know that I need to do the right thing, Jeff, and I will, eventually...' But the years go by and his spiritual arteries are hardening. Every time I see him, not only is he still in his cave, but it gets darker and more forbidding in there.

God has not let him down – he just won't take five steps.

Perhaps those of us who live this way feel that if God really wants us to shape up, then He'll shout loud enough to make us jump. Or maybe He'll wave a flag, pick us up by the ears and spin us around, or... blow some wind, shake the planet, send down some fire...

Yet God is not 'in' all of that. His voice is described in this passage as the 'still small voice' (KJV). Some have translated this as 'the sound of gentle silence'. It is 'qol demama daqqa', the silent sound.

Silent sound? Seems like a contradictory statement – like black white, rich poor or alive dead. Silent sound. But in my experience, the voice of God is just like that: gentle, calm, solidly there, yet – was that really Him? How many times have you thought that you heard God speak, only to spend the next few days considering whether the actual source was your imagination/eating late at night/the devil/wishful thinking?

No wonder the late John Wimber remarked (and I paraphrase) that God is saying a lot to us – we don't seem to hear because He doesn't speak in a way we expect Him to. Preconceptions about the nature of His voice ultimately cause us to become deaf to Him.

Perhaps we don't hear Him more because we are looking for Him to say something new, when actually He may well be bringing us back to a previous statement that we've ignored or disobeyed. Certainly that was Elijah's experience. Once out of the cave, cloak wrapped round his face for fear that he might actually see Yahweh, it's question time again: 'What are you doing here, Elijah?'

Same old question.

Back to square one.

Sometimes we feel as if God has gone silent on us. Perhaps it's good to check to make sure that last time He spoke, we heard and responded.

-     -   -   -   -

Having finally captured Elijah's attention, it was time for God to reveal his strategy.

And what a plan it was too.

It was a totally radical approach – so revolutionary that Elijah had missed it altogether. Elijah thought that God would prompt Ahab and Jezebel to repent and that the nation would follow, but as we've already noted, God was finished with them.

God's plan went like this:

Step one: 'Go back the same way you came, and travel to the wilderness of Damascus. When you arrive there, anoint Hazael to be king of Aram.'

Whether Elijah realised it or not, this was designed to solve the problem of Ahab and Jezebel. The Arameans were called to wage a war upon Israel, behind which flashed the judgment of God; a war in which the king of Israel would be killed and Israel would receive punishment for their awful, heartless and idolatrous crimes. Hazael would become nothing but a puppet to fulfil the will of God. If Elijah would obey, then the plan would be set in motion.

Step two: 'Then anoint Jehu grandson of Nimshi to be king of Israel'.

Elijah would have been shattered, staggered even, to hear this part of God's great idea. This was unbelievable. Perhaps he had at last been driven over the abyss into madness. Why had he fled in terror in the first place? Because he was scared of Ahab and Jezebel. And now listen to God's instruction:

'Anoint another king' (my paraphrase).

Nothing could be more guaranteed to fan the flames of Jezebel's anger to inferno pitch. To anoint Jehu would be to sign his own death warrant - or so it seemed to Elijah.

History shows us clearly what Elijah could never know, except by faith.

He didn't know that Jehu was a man with a heart for renewal and revival.

He didn't know that Jehu was destined to give the order for Jezebel to be thrown out of a high window to her timely death.

He didn't know that Jehu was destined to be the man who oversaw the systematic destruction of Ahab's line of descendants, so that after the reigns of Ahaziah and Jehoram there would be no more coronations for Ahab's descendants.

He didn't know that it would be Jehu who would throw the Tyrian Baal out of Israel, and that even though Jehu would later compromise himself, he was the instrument of God to bring about a massive reform in Israel. Elijah didn't know all this...

Step three: 'and anoint Elisha son of Shaphat from the town of Abel-meholah to replace you as my prophet. Anyone who escapes from Hazael will be killed by Jehu, and those who escape Jehu will be killed by Elisha!'

Having given his strategy for the nation, God now turns to Elijah's personal need – primarily, his need of a friend, a successor; someone whom he could shape so that the prophetic anointing could continue.

Step four: A final encouraging word to the man who spent six weeks in an emotional and actual desert:

> *Yet I will preserve 7,000 others in Israel who have never bowed down to Baal or kissed him!*

Again, God was confirming the truth: Elijah had stood bravely, but not alone. He was to be encouraged by the fact that there was still a faithful remnant who were true to God. He was alone after all.

So God's plan had been given. The big question is: did Elijah obey?

The answer is not, as they say, 'Yes and no.' It is more accurately, 'No... and no... and yes.'

He didn't anoint Hazael.

That would come later, under the ministry of Elisha, and he indeed would become instrumental in the justice programme that God insisted was appropriate for Israel. But it wasn't Elijah who anointed Hazael.

This disobedience is so shocking that evangelical commentators have been loath to concede that Elijah actually got it wrong. The classic writer A.W. Pink actually suggests in his otherwise wonderful book on Elijah that only 'infidels' would suggest that Elijah made a mistake in not holding an anointing service. He argues that Elisha did it eventually, and so that was sufficient.

But what did God say? 'Go back the way you came.... to the Desert of Damascus. *When you get there, anoint Hazael*' (NIV, my emphasis). Now that's very specific and clear, isn't it?

Pink argues that perhaps Elijah did anoint Hazael, but the Bible doesn't record it – although it does carefully document the way Elijah initiated Elisha into the office of prophet by throwing his cloak around him. It isn't enough to say that David was anointed twice, so perhaps Hazael was too. In David's case, *both* anointments are clearly documented in Scripture.

Also, if Hazael was anointed secretly by Elijah, why didn't he immediately become king of Aram, as he did when Elisha anointed him?

Why did *Elisha*, years later, announce to Hazael that 'the Lord had shown him' Hazael was to become king, if they had both been involved in a secret anointing ceremony in the Desert of Damascus years earlier?

And why did Hazael react with such amazement and surprise when Elisha prophesied that he would be king?

The unpalatable fact seems to be that Elijah didn't follow through on stage one.

Moving to stage two, the anointing of Jehu, the answer is 'no' again. And so the evil reign of Ahab continued unabated, and when he was finally killed during battle (a stray Aramean arrow finished him off), Hazael was not on the scene, and Jehu wasn't there, anointed and ready to take over.

Ahab's son, Ahaziah, ruled for two years. He was just like his father. Two more years of the Baals. There would be a brief moment towards the end of Elijah's ministry when the old prophet would challenge the Baal worship by calling down fire upon a hundred of Jehoram's soldiers, and Elijah also prophesied Ahaziah's death – but when that demise came as a result of the king taking a fatal tumble from his Samarian balcony, there was no Jehu waiting in the wings, ready and willing to take the throne. He had not been anointed.

So another descendant of Ahab ascends to the throne. Another son, in fact. This time it was Jehoram – not to be confused with Jehoram of Judah, who became evil by marrying Athaliah, one of Ahab and Jezebel's daughters. Elijah sent a prophetic note across the border to him, condemning him to a painful death of rotting intestines.

Jehoram of Israel was a little better than his brother, but not much. Some minor amendments were made (probably because he was scared stiff that what had happened to his brother and brother-in-law might happen to him). But his eleven-year reign was inconsequential, and he was destined to die at the hands of the next king. During Jehoram's reign Elijah was called away to heaven.

And so thirteen years were wasted.

God's radical plan was not totally thwarted – it was just delayed. God is a redeemer. He can turn our disobedience around to something good in the end.

But the shadow of Ahab's dynasty continued to eclipse Israel.

Then, one great day, the sun broke out. Elisha, now in the full throes of his prophetic office, declared that God had shown him that Hazael was to become king over Aram. (There was no suggestion here that Elijah had told Elisha many years earlier. God had to speak His strategy again.)

It was Elisha who summoned up the bravery to anoint Jehu, right under the nose of the then reigning Jehoram. Elisha was willing to go the full distance with Plan B, and so Jehu ascended to the throne.

The sad implication of all this is that Elijah was a great, mighty, anointed man, but one who was unwilling to go all the way with God when it came to being utterly radical. He saw and experienced so much of the Lord, and dwarfs us by comparison with his great bravery and faith. But the fact remains that he didn't follow through 100% – the threefold strategy of God's plan was met by a mixed response: 'No, no and yes.'

The radical had reached his limits.

Eight:
AFTER SINAI

'So Elijah went and found Elisha son of Shaphat plowing a field. There were twelve teams of oxen in the field, and Elisha was plowing with the twelfth team. Elijah went over to him and threw his cloak across his shoulders and then walked away. Elisha left the oxen standing there, ran after Elijah, and said to him, "First let me go and kiss my father and mother good-bye, and then I will go with you!"

Elijah replied, "Go on back, but think about what I have done to you."

So Elisha returned to his oxen and slaughtered them. He used the wood from the plow to build a fire to roast their flesh. He passed around the meat to the townspeople, and they all ate. Then he went with Elijah as his assistant.' – 1 Kings 19:19-21

'Now there was a man named Naboth, from Jezreel, who owned a vineyard in Jezreel beside the palace of King Ahab of Samaria. One day Ahab said to Naboth, "Since your vineyard is so convenient to my palace, I would like to buy it to use as a vegetable garden. I will give you a better vineyard in exchange, or if you prefer, I will pay you for it."

But Naboth replied, "The Lord forbid that I should give you the inheritance that was passed down by my ancestors."

So Ahab went home angry and sullen because of Naboth's answer. The king went to bed with his face to the wall and refused to eat!

"What's the matter?" his wife Jezebel asked him. "What's made you so upset that you're not eating?"

"I asked Naboth to sell me his vineyard or trade it, but he refused!" Ahab told her.

"Are you the king of Israel or not?" Jezebel demanded. "Get up and eat something, and don't worry about it. I'll get you Naboth's vineyard!"

So she wrote letters in Ahab's name, sealed them with his seal, and sent them to the elders and other leaders of the town where Naboth lived. In her letters she commanded: "Call the citizens together for a time of fasting, and give Naboth a place of honor. And then seat two scoundrels across from him who will accuse him of cursing God and the king. Then take him out and stone him to death."

So the elders and other town leaders followed the instructions Jezebel had written in the letters. They called for a fast and put Naboth at a prominent place before the people. Then the two scoundrels came and sat down across from him. And they accused Naboth before all the people, saying, "He cursed God and the king." So he was dragged outside the town and stoned to death. The town leaders then sent word to Jezebel, "Naboth has been stoned to death."

When Jezebel heard the news, she said to Ahab, "You know the vineyard Naboth wouldn't sell you? Well, you can have it now! He's dead!" So Ahab immediately went down to the vineyard of Naboth to claim it.

But the Lord said to Elijah, "Go down to meet King Ahab of Israel, who rules in Samaria. He will be at Naboth's vineyard in Jezreel, claiming it for himself. Give him this message: 'This is what the Lord says: Wasn't it enough that you killed Naboth? Must you rob him, too? Because you have done this, dogs will lick your blood at the very place where they licked the blood of Naboth!'"

"So, my enemy, you have found me!" Ahab exclaimed to Elijah.

"Yes," Elijah answered, "I have come because you have sold yourself to what is evil in the LORD's sight. So now the LORD says, 'I will bring disaster on you and consume you. I will destroy every one of your male descendants, slave and free alike, anywhere in Israel! I am going to destroy your family as I did the family of Jeroboam son of Nebat and the family of Baasha son of Ahijah, for you have made me very angry and have led Israel into sin.'

And regarding Jezebel, the LORD says, 'Dogs will eat Jezebel's body at the plot of land in Jezreel.'

The members of Ahab's family who die in the city will be eaten by dogs, and those who die in the field will be eaten by vultures."

(No one else so completely sold himself to what was evil in the LORD's sight as Ahab did under the influence of his wife Jezebel. His worst outrage was worshiping idols just as the Amorites had done—the people whom the LORD had driven out from the land ahead of the Israelites.)

But when Ahab heard this message, he tore his clothing, dressed in burlap, and fasted. He even slept in burlap and went about in deep mourning.

Then another message from the LORD came to Elijah: "Do you see how Ahab has humbled himself before me? Because he has done this, I will not do what I promised during his lifetime. It will happen to his sons; I will destroy his dynasty."' - 1 Kings 21:1-29

While Elijah's public ministry and involvement in the ongoing life of Israel continued very spasmodically after he came down from Carmel, his contribution and effectiveness as a national prophet were never fully regained - perhaps a further indication that he had not totally obeyed God's instructions.

That's not to say that his life was without significance after coming down from the mountain of Moses, for his ministry veered into other, fruitful directions.

Elijah and Elisha probably spent a few years investing themselves in a prophetic school, training and shaping others. (We'll look more into that idea in the next chapter.) But the fact is that Elijah faded quickly from the national scene as a direct prophetic spokesman, and he only ministered publicly twice (and sent one prophecy through the postal system) in a period of between ten and fifteen years.

These years were turbulent times for Israel.

During this period, the royal city of Samaria came under siege from Ben-Hadad of Syria, who held the nation to ransom and demanded that Ahab hand over his huge treasury of silver and gold, together with 'the best of his wives and children'. Amazingly, Ahab agreed to these terms, and only resisted when Ben-Hadad increased his demands and insisted that Ahab's furniture be thrown in as part of the deal as well.

Now there's a man with distorted priorities.

Obviously a prophetic voice was needed at this time of threat and calamity – but it was not the voice of Elijah that spoke during this national crisis.

Scripture simply declares that 'a prophet came to Ahab and announced'. This was probably one of the younger prophets from one of the colleges or 'schools of the prophets' that were gradually being re-established at this time.

There followed a battle that included the mustering of some seven thousand Israelite men and was won largely because God helped, and Ben-Hadad and his friends were too busy partying to be a serious strategic threat.

At the moment of truth, the king and the other thirty-two kings who had allied themselves with him were so inebriated that they were almost totally oblivious as to who and where the enemy was. No tactical brilliance was therefore required of the Israelites, as the enemy troops scored an own goal by turning upon one another in confusion, and destroyed themselves by the do-it-yourself method.

After this victory, the anonymous prophet went again to the palace and told Ahab to strengthen and consolidate his defences, warning of another attack to come the following spring. But still there is nothing but silence from Tishbe, home of Elijah.

The young prophet was certainly accurate in his prediction, for spring blossomed, and with it came another attack from Ben-Hadad, who had been falsely advised that Yahweh was only the god of the hills, and not the plains. Ben-Hadad's strategy was, 'We shall fight them on the plains – and beat them.'

Bad theology is a harsh taskmaster.
Yahweh is the God of the universe.

The opposition suffered massive casualties in just one day of fighting. Even those who escaped the battlefield met disaster – thousands were killed when the main wall of the city of Aphek fell on them.

Ahab, however, was always a fool for making unwise treaties. Instead of dealing with Ben-Hadad once and for all, he entered into a trading covenant with the man, and this caused God to commission another unnamed prophet.

God's anger was so stirred that one of the prophets was called to prophetically sentence the king of Israel to death because he 'set free a man [God] determined should die'.

However, it wasn't Elijah who stepped forward
to don the judge's black cap, but rather one of
the 'group of prophets' (1 Kings 20:35).

Through all of this national and international upheaval,
Elijah was silent. So apart from his work behind the scenes,
what *did* he do publicly during those fifteen years?

-　　　-　　　-　　　-　　　-

The infamous Naboth conspiracy took place some
five or six years after the Sinai theophany.

Nothing had changed at the palace: evil still lingered
unchallenged in the hearts of the royal couple. Perhaps Carmel
had momentarily stirred and disturbed Ahab, but not for long.
He had brushed his eye-witness encounter with truth and
power aside. He and Jezebel determined to continue their
selfish, hedonistic lifestyles, ignorant of or oblivious to Yahweh.

Yet while nothing had changed, all was not well with Ahab. In
fact the king was having one of his customary sulking sessions
– one which had driven him to his bed with depression. He was
refusing to eat – a pouting prince with his thumb in his mouth.
The reason for his childish, petulant behaviour was Naboth:
a man of integrity who at least had some level of respect for
the true God and refused to sell his vineyard to the king,
despite the offer of a fair price or a replacement vineyard.

Naboth knew that such a deal was tempting as a business
contract, but it violated God's law: 'No inheritance in Israel is
to pass from one tribe to another, for every Israelite shall keep
the tribal inheritance of their ancestors' (Num. 36:7, NIV).

Enter the spider.

Jezebel was staggered by what she viewed
as her husband's weak behaviour.

What kind of king would allow his moods or actions to be
controlled by a nobody like Naboth? She had a plan. And
once again, the demons smiled on her. It was executed
with brilliant efficiency. It was a glorious setup, with a
little help from her friends, both seen and unseen.

Naboth was confused by the whirlwind of events, but thrilled
and excited all the same. He had been nervous about declining
the king's offer, and he had worried for some while about
possible reprisals or harassment. But now it seemed his fears
were groundless. Apparently, the king had decided to honour
Naboth's integrity. All over Jezreel copies of a royal edict were
pinned, proclaiming a special fast in honour of Naboth.

Think of it. Him, a humble nobody, being invested with
honour by the king and queen of the land. The plan was to
seat him in a place of honour with the elders of the town,
and there the whole city would gather to pay tribute to him.

Naboth shook his head with amazement. It was like a dream;
almost too good to be true. He looked at the sea of smiling faces,
a wave of approval for him. And then everything changed.

The crowd that had been cheering seconds ago were hushed
into an awkward, embarrassed silence. From the back of the
packed town square, the voices of two men were raised – their
bony fingers pointing up towards the platform of honour,
where a man who had been so happy and proud just seconds
ago now sat white faced, with skin taut and eyes wide. 'He
cursed God and king! He's a traitor, and deserves to die.'

The crowds surely knew. They knew that it wasn't true.

Naboth was a good, honest man. They also knew that the
accusers were scoundrels; thugs in the pay of someone

very, very powerful. But what could they do? Solemnly, the elders of the town, who had found themselves somewhat richer in the last few hours, courtesy of the palace, stood and condemned the man whom they had just honoured to be taken out and stoned to death.

The crowds stood silent; every man wanting to shout, to protest, to *do* something. But they said nothing.

The now-screaming Naboth was led away, probably already a madman because of the soaring joy and the plummeting agony of the day. Dragged away to face the pelting of the stones that would crack and break and bruise and bloody his frail body, until finally the aches that screamed from every cell within him would be mercifully silenced. And then they took the dead man's sons and stoned them to death as well, so that there would be no inheritance complications to prevent 'an unknown backer' from purchasing Naboth's fateful vineyard. It was a bad job well done.

Poor Naboth had been right.

It had been too good to be true.

-     -   -   -   -

God wants us to seek His kingdom – and His righteousness.

But contrary to popular belief, righteousness is not just about personal integrity and holiness, but is more broadly about things in society and culture being right.

It is not right, in God's eyes, when the poor are exploited, when the widows are ignored, when the planet is misused (because we don't own planet Earth, but are stewards of what God has created and has lent to us), when innocents are trafficked, or when multinational corporations raid the pension funds of their employees and leave them vulnerable, and also because of the greed of a few. God wants a just society, and so when we insist that God loves justice, we are not just talking about a judicial system with integrity, but about things being done in a fair and right way. The root word for righteousness, *tsdq*, is used to describe pathways that are straight (Psa. 23:3) and weights and measures that are correct (Lev. 19:36; Deut. 25:15). God is also the judge, *spt*, who arbitrates, makes judgments, and defends the legal rights of the oppressed.

All of this means that our giving to areas of need is an act of justice – and not just charity – and that some of the major issues of our day should not be rendered as 'political' and seen to be outside of the remit of the Church, but the Church needs to speak to these issues because God loves and upholds righteousness.

When God introduced the call to holiness to His people, it was a call to a personal and social ethic that included caring for the poor, caring for the elderly, looking after those with disabilities, feeding the poor, caring for the marginalised, and doing business with honesty – a call that reflected his own dependable character.

But often the people of God have prioritised personal piety and ignored social justice. As Israelite society shifted from its agricultural roots to a more urban and commercial society, the prophets cried out against wrong relationships, corrupted by the twin viruses of greed and injustice. God's Law envisioned a peaceful society in which each person rested safely under his own vine and fig tree (1 Kings 4:25; Micah 4:4). Yet when Israel became prosperous, a wealthy upper class developed. The old values embedded in the law of mutual aid and sharing were replaced by selfishness and indifference to the poor. Thus Amos, in Jeroboam's day, cried out against oppression of the poor by the rich (Amos 2:6-7), against indifference toward the hungry (6:3-6), and against corruption in the courts (2:7; 8:6), as well as against blatant immorality (2:7).

The prophets further develop the priestly belief expressed in the law that the holiness of God demands social justice (Isa. 5:16; Jer. 31:31-34; Ezek. 28:22; 38:23). God manifests His holiness by moving humans to righteous living, by which they model His values in their communal life and mediate a true knowledge of the Holy One to the nations (Isa. 42:1,6). God will not hear the prayers of those who ignore the cries of the poor (Isa. 1:10-17). To care for the poor sits at the very heart of what it genuinely means to know the Lord, and is therefore true religion, as in the case of King Josiah, described by the prophet Jeremiah and picked up later by James in the New Testament: "He defended the cause of the poor and needy, and so all went well. Is that not what it means to know me?" declares the LORD' (Jer. 22:16, NIV), 'Religion that God our Father accepts as pure and faultless is this: to look after orphans and widows in their distress and to keep oneself from being polluted by the world' (James 1:27, NIV).

Elsewhere in Scripture, we see God's heart raging against injustice. Nathan the prophet confronted King David about his treatment of poor Uriah (2 Sam. 12:7). The wisdom literature similarly calls for justice (Prov. 16:12, 31:4-5; Eccl. 5:8).

And so, in 'seeking first the kingdom and His righteousness' we must engage with these complex but vital issues.

-    -   -   -   -

At the palace, a glad and smiling king got up from his tear-stained bed. He washed and dressed and celebrated with a sumptuous meal, and blessed the day that his father had arranged his marriage to the fair lady Jezebel.

I wonder whether Elijah agonised over the shift in his ministry away from the glare of public profile.

During those six long years of silence, did he ever wistfully reminisce over the 'glory days' of national significance? Did he ever wonder if he was now consigned to the scrap heap of half-obedience – a blazing sword in the hand of God once, now feeling like a blunt stick, yesterday's man?

What kind of agonies come to those who have stood in the spotlight of fame, recognition or influence, who suddenly find that the stage lights have dimmed, the scenery has rotted and faded, and the auditorium is empty, the crowds have gone, and they've taken their intoxicating applause with them? All that's left are yellowing posters and a few dated photographs.

It's interesting that during the Naboth narrative Elijah is referred to as 'Elijah, the prophet from Tishbe' – almost as if a reintroduction is necessary. He has gone back home to the humble village where it all started – obscurity again.

However, like Samson, whose hair began to grow again and who had one last burst of blessing before death, so Elijah was destined to blaze a trail one more time before handing over the job to one younger and stronger. The king must be rebuked – justice must be done.

The oppressed must be defended.

And Elijah had to face his fears, because the call made it clear.

He had to go to the palace again.

Something of God's mercy and kindness can be seen in this recommissioning of Elijah. Even though it seems he was unwilling to go all the way, still God enabled him to recover some of his confidence by providing him with a mission that he would be able to respond to fully. It was, after all, familiar ground.

He had confronted Ahab face to face before. The stage would be lit, albeit temporarily, a couple more times.

-       -   -   -   -

It was the joy that comes when you get something new, or when you reach a goal: a quiet, luscious sense of satisfaction. So Ahab felt as he strolled regally around the 'Traitor's' vineyard – now the title deeds for the place were safely in the royal purse. Like a child who has screamed and begged and manipulated until he has finally got his own way, and then smiles with self-congratulation, so Ahab smiled.

Briefly.

Suddenly the vines parted behind him and a voice bellowed out, insistent and throaty, demanding a response. The king turned around; a sense of déjà vu causing his mind to spin too.

He knew that voice, but it was a sound from the past – an uncomfortable echo from yesteryear. No, it couldn't be...

Ahab looked into the face of his old enemy – Elijah.

It was a prophetic curse. Rhythmic, lilting, haunting even: *Ilaratzachta vegam yarashta*.' The closest English translation, according to Lance Pierson, is, 'So you're a con man as well as a cut-throat.'

This was the third slap in the face that Ahab received from God: first a slap with a drought because of spiritual idolatry; then a rebuke with a suspended death sentence for his disobedience and rashness in covenant-making with demonised kings; and now, a smack once more for oppressing the poor.

It's worth pausing for a moment here to take note of the rather obvious fact that God is interested in both the political and the so-called spiritual. With God, there is no distinction. Those who would like the Church to confine itself to the winning of souls only and to be silent in matters of politics, have neglected to read Scripture. Yet such a dualistic viewpoint ('concentrate on the spiritual, ignore the secular') still pervades, at least in a few circles. In an environment where the Church practises a pathological fear of all things politically controversial, we will never be able to cry out on behalf of the poor and oppressed – and the Bible tells us that the gospel is for them. Oppression and injustice cause the heart of God to rage with terrifying anger – and they should make us angry as well. We need to mix genuine, caring compassion with our activism. When we cease to defend the rights of the oppressed, we become a hard-faced group of moralists – passionate about our agendas, but with no heart.

With love and tears, but with strategy and clarity, the church must say to governments, to certain multi-national corporations, and indeed to all who oppress: *Ilaratzachta vegam yarashta.* (Or, more helpfully, a contemporary and more understandable version thereof.)

As love and truth mingle, then the Church becomes the incarnate conscience that God has surely called it to be.

Ahab, now instantly robbed of the joy that he had felt as the new master of the vineyard, immediately tried to distract Elijah with a few cunning, well-chosen words: 'Have you caught up with me, my enemy?'

After the long years, Ahab immediately drew thick verbal
battle lines afresh; invoking memories of Jezebel's vow
of long ago – a vow that made Elijah an enemy still. Is
there perhaps a hint of mockery here too, in the question,
'Have you caught up with me?' Perhaps he was taunting
the prophet who had been sheltering in obscurity for too
long. 'Where have you been, Elijah? Long time, no see.
After all these years, you've finally managed to find me.'

Elijah didn't flinch. He made no attempt to explain himself
or to justify his long silence. He just launched into the bad
news – there was no good news available for Ahab at this
stage of his life. After denouncing the king as one who
had 'sold himself' (as one who sells himself utterly into
slavery) to do evil in God's sight, Elijah delivered a sentence
in two counts. Let's take a time-warp approach so we can
see the power of the prophetic utterance more clearly:

Part one – the promise:

> *I will bring disaster on you and consume you. I will
> destroy every one of your male descendants, slave and
> free alike, anywhere in Israel! I am going to destroy your
> family as I did the family of Jeroboam son of Nebat
> and the family of Baasha son of Ahijah, for you have
> made me very angry and have led Israel into sin.*
>
> (1 Kings 21:21-22)

The fulfilment: About twelve years later, Jehu would instigate
a purge that would let everyone know that 'not a word...
spoken against the house of Ahab will fail' (NIV). The
seventy remaining descendants of Ahab, together with
all his chief men, close friends and priests, would all be
put to the sword, their heads put in baskets and sent to
Jezreel. Then all the relatives of Ahab's son Ahaziah would
be slaughtered by the well of Beth Eked – 42 of them.

Finally, Jehu was destined to go to Samaria, and wipe out any and every remaining member of Ahab's family – a thorough and total purge.

Part two – the promise:

> *'Dogs will eat Jezebel's body at the plot of land in Jezreel.' The members of Ahab's family who die in the city will be eaten by dogs, and those who die in the field will be eaten by vultures.*
>
> (1 Kings 21:23-24)

This wasn't the first time dogs had been used as agents by God to judge royalty. Elijah prophesied that Ahab's house would be like Jeroboam's and Baasha's houses. Jeroboam had already gone down in history as an idolater whose descendants were eaten by dogs. It is written of Jeroboam: 'the LORD struck him down and he died' (2 Chron. 13:20). The very mention of his name would have brought an icy chill to Ahab's heart – a reminder from contemporary history that God would perform what He had said.

Then, the mention of Baasha drove the point home like a sharp knife. He was another one who had been consumed by dogs: 'Dogs will eat those belonging to Baasha who die in the city' (1 Kings 16:4, NIV).

The fulfilment: Again, it would be some twelve years later. By this time Ahab would be dead, succeeded by his evil son Ahaziah, with Jezebel as Queen Mother. She would have known that the end had come as Jehu walked through the gates of the Jezreel country house.

News had reached her that Jehu had just killed Ahaziah. The great purge had begun. She did her manipulative best to save her own neck, painting her eyes and fixing her hair (perhaps she could use her old charms seductively one last time). When the beauty treatment failed, she even tried a last attempt at undermining Jehu, yelling out of the window at him, 'Have you come in peace, you murderer? You're just like Zimri, who murdered his master!' (2 Kings 9:31).

The desperate Queen Mother was resorting to name-calling.

It was a doomed scheme, however.

She was thrown out of the high window by a couple of her own servants, who swiftly decided that it would be politically expedient to side with Jehu. Considering the evil smear that was Jezebel's life, it is worth reporting the details of her demise in full – macabre and sickening though they are:

> So they threw her down, and some of her blood spattered the wall and the horses as they trampled her underfoot... when they went out to bury her, they found nothing except her skull, her feet and her hands. They went back and told Jehu, who said, 'This is the word of the LORD that he spoke through his servant Elijah the Tishbite: on the plot of ground at Jezreel dogs will devour Jezebel's flesh. Jezebel's body will be like dung on the ground in the plot at Jezreel, so that no one will be able to say, 'This is Jezebel'.
>
> (2 Kings 9:33,35–37, NIV)

–   –   –   –   –

When Ahab heard Elijah's words of promised judgment, he knew he was a dead man walking – and incredibly, for once in his life, he repented. It was a thorough job; one that, perhaps even more surprisingly, God responded to warmly. He tore his clothes, fasted, lay in sackcloth and 'went around meekly'. And after all the evil, the child killing, God showed him a measure of mercy, determining that judgments would fall on his house rather than on him directly. The disaster was delayed by his repentant heart.

What a God we serve, who seizes on even a glimmer of repentance and shows mercy wherever and whenever He can.

But this is not a 'happy ever after' story for Ahab. Within three short years he had gone back to his old ways, despising God's prophets and surviving again by political manipulation.

Ahab's downfall came because he seemed unable or unwilling to learn his lessons, seemingly going around in ever-vicious circles. He would realise the truth for a while, but then slip back into old patterns, never bringing his will into line with what he knew to be right.

The battle that had raged for years between Elijah and Ahab was over – they were never to meet again.

Judgment day for this prince of evil came on the battlefield. A 'stray' Aramean arrow penetrated his armour, and despite being propped up in his chariot for the rest of the day (a last desperate propaganda exercise), he died from the massive loss of blood that 'spilled onto the floor of his chariot'.

They took the royal chariot to the splendid palace at Samaria – Ahab's old ivory tower.

There they washed it in the prostitutes' pool in the palace grounds, where all battle weapons and chariots were taken for cleaning.

And Scripture notes one further little detail.

The dogs came by, and licked up his blood.

–　　–　　–　　–　　–

Ahab was gone, but still Elijah had not anointed Jehu, God's man for the hour.

And so Ahab's son came to power. He didn't enjoy an easy reign. Moab, the subject kingdom which lay east of the Jordan, had decided that it had had enough of Israel's tax demands. For some forty-six years Moab had been required to contribute one hundred thousand lamb fleeces and one hundred thousand ram skins every year to Israel's treasury. This was a massively heavy burden, so they staged a revolution and rebelled against their oppressors. Apparently it didn't occur to King Ahaziah to seek the Lord – and so, like his father before him, he bowed the knee to the Baals.

The situation came to a head about four years after the Naboth incident, following a domestic accident which left the king injured. He fell off his own balcony. How, or why, Scripture doesn't tell us. Some have speculated that he did so in a drunken stupor.

Whatever the cause of his fall, the effect was serious. He was badly injured, and so hurriedly sent a messenger off to Ekron, which had an extensive population of fortune-tellers. It was the insect god Baal-Zebub from whom he sought counsel. He didn't seek healing, but revelation. His question was simple: 'Will I live, or will I die?'

Enter the angel of the Lord, calling Elijah to active service once more.

The king of Israel had especially offended Yahweh by consulting with Baal-Zebub, chief demon of demons, the lord of the flies, the god of the dung heap. The incredulity that reverberated in the heart of Yahweh is echoed three times in the call of Elijah, as he cries out to a king wallowing in refuse and sewage, 'Is there no God in Israel?'

The verdict was stark and stern. Elijah had intercepted
Ahaziah's messengers as they urged their horses on
towards Philistia's dung heap. They had wondered
why they had felt compelled to stop at the beckoning
of the leather-faced man, seemingly just another
Bedouin peasant, but they had stopped anyway.

And then they understood.

It was Elijah, the man who had become a
thorn in the now dead Ahab's side.

He had come out of obscurity again, to give the new king
trouble. His message was bad news: no invitation to the
king to repent; no drought to bring him to his senses.

As a son of Ahab he should have known better. His father had
been a pictorial illustration of depravity, and his mother was
still yet the lingering black widow who loved the fly god.

There was no room for misunderstanding in
Elijah's words: 'Tell the king he will die.'

The king was understandably taken aback by the rude
intervention of his father's old enemy, but there was no response
of thoughtful repentance, in the hope that God might hold out
some hope of reprieve as He had offered, without success, to Ahab.

Instead he decided to fight – to fight Elijah. And to pick a
fight with Elijah was to pick a fight with the living God,
who is, as Hebrews 12:29 puts it, 'a consuming fire'.

–   –   –   –   –

The mounted commando unit had been carefully
briefed for the mission. Some of the younger, more
headstrong among them had laughed at the fact that

fifty of their number – fifty of the most elite troops in the land – were required for the arrest of just one man.

They were eager, excited, ready to get into a mission that had a certain guarantee of success. But there were some who were unable to hide the pensive feelings that filled their hearts. They were old enough to remember Elijah from the glory days. The story of Carmel had been part of the fabric of their childhood, and however limited their understanding, they knew that the man had some kind of power. But this was not a time for fearful questioning.

Orders had been issued. There was a job to be done.

Some people wish that the next part of Elijah's story had never been written. The facts are blunt, and hideous. Elijah and Elisha were camped out on a hillside: a sure vantage point from where they would be able to see all comers. The captain of the royal commando issued a command to the man of God: 'the king has commanded you to come down with us' (2 Kings 1:9).

Elijah's response was pointed, and the macabre miracle that followed even more so. 'If I am a man of God,' he said, 'let fire come down from heaven and destroy you and your fifty men' (1 Kings 1:10). The unpalatable fact is this: an instant cremation took place. White-hot heat that vaporised flesh flashed from the sky, incinerating the entire platoon in a second.

Like the divine ignition that broke out against the complaining Israelites at Taberah (Num. 11:3) and then again during the rebellion of Korah, when 250 were judged in a moment, so God decisively dealt with the arrogant captain and his men.

As if this wasn't enough, the whole process is then repeated. The incredibly pig-headed Ahaziah sent out another posse on what proved to be a kamikaze mission, because they met exactly the same fate.

One hundred smouldering mounds and the foul, sickly odour of scorched flesh were all that remained to testify that these crack fighters had ever existed.

Back at the palace, Ahaziah sat unmoved, and sent out platoon number three. The commander of the third outfit was a little more sensible than his dead comrades.

He fell on his knees before Elijah and pleaded for mercy – an unusual military strategy. At this point the angel of God returned and assured Elijah that it would be safe for him to go with the officer and confront the bull-headed king face to face. The meeting is hurriedly arranged, and Ahaziah holds the most depressing audience of his life. Elijah simply marches in and repeats the word already spoken; 'Yes, king – you are still going to die.' And he did – after a reign of less than two years.

Did Elijah (and God!) overstep the mark by arranging an instant cremation for a hundred innocent men? It does seem a little extreme, to say the least, to torch men who after all were simply obeying orders. But we need to take a step back and think again. Ahaziah was doing far more than issuing a warrant for the arrest of Elijah. He was trying to throw a punch at God Himself. He was endeavouring to maintain the awful horrors of Baal worship: child sacrifice, sexual deviancy and apostasy. How many thousands of innocents would lose their lives, either to death or degradation, if the notion that 'there was no God in Israel' became popular belief? The stakes were massively high. A few were judged in order to grab the nation's attention, so that the whole nation would not fall under God's curse.

We should also remember the attitude of the third captain, who very sensibly climbed down off his arrogant high horse and was spared as a result. If he did this, presumably the other two unfortunate captains before him could have done the same.

It was Elijah's last public act in the national life of Israel, although there was one other incident which we shall look at very briefly, when Elijah sent an international prophecy by mail.

The letter was addressed to Jehoram, the King of Judah – not Jehoram King of Israel. (They both reigned at the same time, adding to the confusion, and to make it worse they were related by marriage.) Jehoram of Judah had made the incredible mistake of marrying one of Ahab and Jezebel's daughters, Athaliah. When you marry the daughter of such a mother, it's likely you'll get tainted in the process.

Judah's Jehoram began to follow the old and depressing road of Baalism, murder and all the rest. At this point there were actually two kings leading Judah (not an unusual situation – kings often rode 'tandem' during the hand-over period), so Jehoshaphat and Jehoram ruled together. This must have been the case, because Jehoshaphat outlived Elijah – and Elijah didn't send a letter from the grave. It was during the transitional period that the letter was written.

Jehoram had no excuse – his father Jehoshaphat had been a good man. Elijah's letter pronounced a curse on his people, his children, his wives and his possessions, and finally announced that he would die of a disease of the bowel.

Six years later, after a two-year illness, the unrepentant king died in agony. He died unmourned.

Once again Elijah's prophetic ministry had hit the target dead centre with devastating accuracy – although he never saw the fulfilment of that particular prophetic word. In fact, he probably left the letter with Elisha, who either delivered it personally or had one of the younger 'sons of the prophets' act as postman. By the time Jehoram went down with terminal intestinal disease, Elijah was long gone.

So Elijah's public ministry drew to a close.

At the beginning of this chapter I remarked that his caseload wasn't especially heavy for the long fifteen-year period between Carmel and his translation.

So what else did he do with his time?

I believe that he probably laboured in the rebuilding and reviving of the prophetic colleges that began to flourish again during that period. These close-knit communities, which ate (but not necessarily lived) together were usually headed up by a chief known as the 'Father'. They were not monastic in the traditional sense – Elisha performed a miracle for 'The wife of a man from the company of the prophets' (2 Kings 4:1, NIV) – but they did live in community.

So much did they flourish under Elisha's later direction that one of the schools had to build a new community to house the growing numbers.

They travelled around in processions, playing lyres, tambourines, flutes and harps, dancing and shouting their prophetic utterances. Samuel was a leader of one of these early guilds (1 Sam. 19:20).

They were so filled with an infectious enthusiasm for Yahweh that occasionally even the unwitting spectator would fall under the prophetic anointing.

Their effect upon the young Saul after being anointed for kingship was remarkable. Samuel declared that after meeting with a school he would be 'changed into a different person' (1 Sam. 10:6), and: 'they saw a group of prophets coming towards them. Then the Spirit of God came powerfully upon Saul' (1 Sam. 10:10). Apparently the schools provided a launching pad and home base for leading itinerant prophets, gathering together for consultation and debriefing whenever the itinerants returned home from their journeys.

Jezebel almost succeeded in wiping out these guilds, but originally there must have been many schools, because the double agent Obadiah succeeded in hiding two schools away without the Queen even noticing.

However, these two were the only schools that remained. In the fifteen-year period after Carmel, the schools doubled in size until there were some two hundred, perhaps in three schools, one of which may have settled in the Carmel area. These schools were to survive and outlive those who plotted to wipe them out – so Elijah's investment must have been well placed.

It's possible that they survived for hundreds of years.

There are hints of New Testament guilds in the book of Acts. Agabus, the man who only prophesied twice (famine and the arrest of Paul), was probably part of a Jerusalem-based guild that travelled to Antioch (Acts 11:27).

Agabus was no strange lone wolf. He was a man in relationship, and he prophesied out of that secure context. Perhaps Elijah lectured his 'sons' long and hard about the perils of lonely ministry – and his teaching legacy lived on right through to the New Testament Church.

Thus the budding prophets became known as the 'sons of the prophets', expressing something of the family spirit that developed between them.

It's a title that Amos refers to some ninety years later: 'I was neither a prophet nor the son of a prophet' (Amos 7:14, NIV).

And in addition to his work with the schools, Elijah invested a great deal into his friendship with the budding successor, Elisha.

Elisha evidently came from a rich family – he was ploughing with six oxen when he received his call, which is the cultural equivalent of driving a shiny new Mercedes.

Elijah had known nothing of the protected environment that affluence can create. He lived a rough-and-ready, hand-to-mouth existence. After all, he did come from a Bedouin background. The contrast between the two men was great.

But Elisha had a kingdom value system: he knew that to follow the call of God would result in a life far more significant and dynamic than the easy life of the son of a rich family.

He turned his back on comfort and security, and began a new life of learning with the camel-skinned Elijah as his master.

And the call of God was a call to serving. It always is.

Elisha is known as Elijah's 'attendant', 'servant' or 'assistant' (1 Kings 19:21) who would 'pour water on the hands' of his master (2 Kings 3:11, NIV). This hand-washing routine was normally only performed by women in the culture of the day, but such was the servant heart of the prophet-in-the-making that he was willing to do anything to serve and bless.

Elisha also served as a faithful traveling companion who wouldn't go away; a strategic counter-balance to Elijah's tendency to retreat into isolation when under pressure.

Before Elijah was finally taken away from Elisha, he asked the younger man a question: 'What do you want me to do for you?'

Elisha responded like a true son in the faith, by asking for the traditional inheritance of the first-born son: 'Give me a double portion of your spirit.'

These two men had forged a solid gold friendship over the ten years they were together.

They were more than colleagues – friends, even.

They were like father and son.

So much had Elijah impacted his assistant that now, when they were about to be parted, Elisha basically says, 'I want to be like you, father – only twice as powerful.'

No rebuke or correction comes from Elijah; no pseudo-humble disclaimer: 'Don't ask to be like me, son. You should emulate God alone.' No, Elijah knew that through all his successes and failures, God had been with him, anointing, shaping, developing him, and now he is a man worthy of being copied.

Truly, Elijah the loner had died on the eerie mountainside of Sinai.

A team player had emerged.

He was about to leave, but he had built well in Elisha, his son, and in the schools of prophets, his true sons in the faith. Now all that remained was a final farewell tour to say goodbye to the schools. The time was drawing near for the great man to go on to higher things.

Nine:
CURTAIN AND ENCORE

'When the LORD was about to take Elijah up to heaven in a whirlwind, Elijah and Elisha were traveling from Gilgal. And Elijah said to Elisha, "Stay here, for the LORD has told me to go to Bethel."

But Elisha replied, "As surely as the LORD lives and you yourself live, I will never leave you!" So they went down together to Bethel.

The group of prophets from Bethel came to Elisha and asked him, "Did you know that the LORD is going to take your master away from you today?"

"Of course I know," Elisha answered. "But be quiet about it."

Then Elijah said to Elisha, "Stay here, for the LORD has told me to go to Jericho."

But Elisha replied again, "As surely as the LORD lives and you yourself live, I will never leave you." So they went on together to Jericho.

Then the group of prophets from Jericho came to Elisha and asked him, "Did you know that the LORD is going to take your master away from you today?"

"Of course I know," Elisha answered. "But be quiet about it."

Then Elijah said to Elisha, "Stay here, for the LORD has told me to go to the Jordan River."

But again Elisha replied, "As surely as the LORD lives and you yourself live, I will never leave you." So they went on together.

Fifty men from the group of prophets also went and watched from a distance as Elijah and Elisha stopped beside the Jordan River. Then Elijah folded his cloak together and struck the water with it. The river divided, and the two of them went across on dry ground!

When they came to the other side, Elijah said to Elisha, "Tell me what I can do for you before I am taken away."

And Elisha replied, "Please let me inherit a double share of your spirit and become your successor."

"You have asked a difficult thing," Elijah replied. "If you see me when I am taken from you, then you will get your request. But if not, then you won't."

As they were walking along and talking, suddenly a chariot of fire appeared, drawn by horses of fire. It drove between the two men, separating them, and Elijah was carried by a whirlwind into heaven. Elisha saw it and cried out, "My father! My father! I see the chariots and charioteers of Israel!" And as they disappeared from sight, Elisha tore his clothes in distress.

Elisha picked up Elijah's cloak, which had fallen when he was taken up. Then Elisha returned to the bank of the Jordan River. He struck the water with Elijah's cloak and cried out, "Where is the LORD, the God of Elijah?" Then the river divided, and Elisha went across.

When the group of prophets from Jericho saw from a distance what happened, they exclaimed, "Elijah's spirit rests upon Elisha!" And they went to meet him and bowed to the ground before him. "Sir," they said, "just say the word and fifty of our strongest men will search the wilderness for your master. Perhaps the Spirit of the LORD has left him on some mountain or in some valley."

"No," Elisha said, "don't send them." But they kept urging him until they shamed him into agreeing, and he finally said, "All right, send

them." So fifty men searched for three days but did not find Elijah. Elisha was still at Jericho when they returned. "Didn't I tell you not to go?" he asked.' – 2 Kings 2:1-18

'Six days later Jesus took Peter and the two brothers, James and John, and led them up a high mountain to be alone. As the men watched, Jesus' appearance was transformed so that his face shone like the sun, and his clothes became as white as light. Suddenly, Moses and Elijah appeared and began talking with Jesus.

Peter exclaimed, "Lord, it's wonderful for us to be here! If you want, I'll make three shelters as memorials—one for you, one for Moses, and one for Elijah."

But even as he spoke, a bright cloud overshadowed them, and a voice from the cloud said, "This is my dearly loved Son, who brings me great joy. Listen to him." The disciples were terrified and fell face down on the ground.

Then Jesus came over and touched them. "Get up," he said. "Don't be afraid." And when they looked up, Moses and Elijah were gone, and they saw only Jesus.' – Matthew 17:1-8

A decade of friendship had been forged between them: 3,000 days and nights of laughter, tears and training as Elisha had shadowed the great man who was also his father and friend.

How many times had Elisha sat enthralled as he heard one more time about the blaze of Carmel?

What anger had raged in his heart, clenching his fists and furrowing his brow, when he had heard the story of poor, innocent, noble Naboth.

Perhaps Elisha had wept openly when he heard about the agony of Sinai, when his master had almost lost his grip on life and sanity - hope put to death, then resurrected again when God walked by.

Ten long years to get to that place where each man could almost tell the other's thoughts, anticipate the other's words, predict the other's responses.

And so now Elisha must have known that something epic was taking place as they began their tour of the schools, beginning at Gilgal, then seven miles south onto Bethel, and then downhill to Jericho, the last stage of the journey.

It seemed like all those with a prophetic heart knew.

Elijah was going to be taken away.

At each place, a prophet told Elisha, 'Your master is leaving,' and they seemed to want to make a fuss about it, but though he knew they were right, he wanted to guard the older man's emotions; to protect him from a succession of tearful, heart-rending farewells. So his response was simply: 'Hold your peace.'

This tour was not just to say goodbye. The two men were in fact doing just exactly what they had been doing for the last ten years: building up the schools. Elijah was about to leave the earth, but such was the order and rhythm of his life that he continued his regular routine. No special time was needed to make peace with God and man. He lived as a man ready to die at any time. He was like John Wesley who, when asked what he would do if he knew he had just three days to live, replied: 'I should just do the work which I had already planned to do: ministering in one place; meeting my preachers in another; lodging in yet another, till the moment came that I was called to yield my spirit back to Him who gave it.'

That's the way to live.

So at last, with fifty of the sons trailing a way behind,
they came to Jordan, where 555 years previously Israel
had celebrated the God who was bigger than Pharaoh.
There were two final steps to take before God called
Elijah to his final reward: a miracle and a mantle.

Elijah took off his cloak, rolled it up, and slapped the muddy
waters of the Jordan. As the swirling waters began to boil
and recede, drawn back by an invisible hand, Elisha saw
completely his place in history. He recognised that the God
of Moses, the God of Joshua, the God of father Elijah, was
also his God. As the waters submitted to a slap, Elisha tasted
personal destiny. But as they walked through the parted
waters without fear, there was one final amen to come.

'I'm about to be taken from you. What special favour can I do
for you?' Elijah asked. And the younger, balding man did not
hesitate to ask for a double portion of his spirit. Elijah's response
seems a little strange at first glance: 'If you see me when I am
taken from you, it will be yours – otherwise it will not' (NIV).
Elijah wasn't playing games here: heads-I-win-tails-you-lose.

It was vital that Elisha saw the horsemen and chariots of Israel.

There would be many trials to come.

Times when he would need to recall the day when God's
angels touched down on earth and took a faithful man home.

Times when he would need to remember that there
is far more to see than most human eyes see.

In 2 Kings 6:17, he later had to pray for his own servant,
'Give him eyes to see what I see' (my paraphrase). I believe
that Elisha's ability to see the unseen – his vision of faith

– was sparked by the way in which his master departed.
School was in session for Elisha until the very last moment.

And so they came, those angels of God, breathtaking and
awesome: a whirlwind and a chariot of fire. The man who
had known the elation of success and a depression that cried
out for death was lifted up by the God whom he had loved.

Jezebel thrown *down* to the dogs; the peasant
from Gilead lifted *up* to a divine embrace.

Certainly he was no angel. He made too many mistakes
for that – just like the rest of us. His life was an epic
story of the ordinary kissed by the Eternal.

Of course there was to be a great encore.

At the time of Christ, there was still an expectation that Elijah
would return. Even today the Passover celebration includes
a spare cup for the prophet, just in case he should choose to
arrive. Some thought that John, and later Jesus, was Elijah
returned. In a sense, John the Baptist picked up Elijah's ministry,
calling the people back to God, preparing the way of the
Lord. That's why Jesus called John 'Elijah'. This doesn't mean
that John was Elijah reincarnate, for John said emphatically
that he wasn't Elijah, but he carried the same mantle.

But Elijah was to appear on the earth one more time, on the
Mount of Transfiguration, where, together with Moses, he
talked with the Lord Jesus while the disciples ran around
in manic circles trying to organise a building programme.

Who knows what they talked about?

Is it possible that, as Jesus faced the final great
step of obedience, Elijah, who did wonderfully but
stopped short of God's total best, encouraged his
Lord to go the whole way, to pay the final price?

Perhaps one day we will know.

What we do know is that this ordinary man, who
was 'just like us', was given an encore of honour
during those transfiguration moments.

—   —   —   —   —

The whirlwind subsided, and the swirling sands began
to thin and settle. Elisha, his heart pounding, picked
himself up off the soft sand where he had pushed
his body down as the angels of God came.

As he stood to his feet, he knew: the shooting star
that was Elijah was gone. And the condition for him
to receive the double portion had been fulfilled.

He had seen Elijah go.

He had seen the chariots and their riders
- warriors from another world.

It was time for work.

Courses and seminars

Waverley Abbey College

Publishing and media

Conference facilities

Transforming lives

CWR's vision is to enable people to experience personal transformation through applying God's Word to their lives and relationships.

Our Bible-based training and resources help people around the world to:
• Grow in their walk with God
• Understand and apply Scripture to their lives
• Resource themselves and their church
• Develop pastoral care and counselling skills
• Train for leadership
• Strengthen relationships, marriage and family life and much more.

Our insightful writers provide daily Bible reading notes and other resources for all ages, and our experienced course designers and presenters have gained an international reputation for excellence and effectiveness.

CWR's Training and Conference Centres in Surrey and East Sussex, England, provide excellent facilities in idyllic settings – ideal for both learning and spiritual refreshment.

CWR Applying God's Word to everyday life and relationships

CWR, Waverley Abbey House,
Waverley Lane, Farnham,
Surrey GU9 8EP, UK

Telephone: **+44 (0)1252 784700**
Email: **info@cwr.org.uk**
Website: **www.cwr.org.uk**

Registered Charity No. 294387
Company Registration No. 1990308